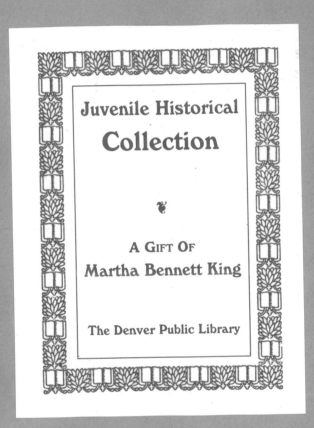

Very Truly Yours,
Charles L. Dodgson,

ALIAS

Lewis Carroll

Very Truly Yours, Charles L. Dodgson, ALIAS Lewis Carroll

A BIOGRAPHY BY LISA BASSETT

LOTHROP, LEE & SHEPARD BOOKS
NEW YORK

Extracts from *The Letters of Lewis Carroll,* ed. by Morton N. Cohen with Roger Lancelyn Green. © Morton Norton Cohen and Roger Lancelyn Green 1978; letters © The Executors of the C. L. Dodgson Estate 1978. The Selection Preface & Notes © Morton N. Cohen and Roger Lancelyn Green, 1978. Reprinted by permission of Oxford University Press, Inc.

Extracts from *The Letters of Lewis Carroll* by permission of The Trustees of the Charles Lutwidge Dodgson Estate, Mr. Morton Cohen, and Macmillan London Ltd.

Quotations from *The Diaries of Lewis Carroll* by permission of The Trustees of the Charles Lutwidge Dodgson Estate.

Extracts from *Reminiscences of a Specialist* by Greville McDonald by permission of Allen & Unwin.

Extracts from *Lewis Carroll: An Illustrated Biography* by permission of Constable Publishers and Derek Hudson.

Extracts from *Ellen Terry's Memoirs* by Ellen Terry, copyright 1932, by permission of G. P. Putnam's Sons.

Quotation from "Lewis Carroll" by Harry R. Mileham, *The Times,* 2 January 1932, by permission of Times Newspapers Limited.

"'Alice' Manuscript, a British Treasure, bought for America" of April 4, 1928. Copyright © 1928 by The New York Times Company. Reprinted by permission.

Extracts from "Alice's Recollections of Carrollian Days" from *Cornhill Magazine,* Vol. LXXIII, by permission of John Murray (Publishers) Ltd.

"To Me He Was Mr. Dodgson," by E. M. Rowell. Copyright © 1943 by Harper's Magazine. All rights reserved. Reprinted from the February issue by special permission.

Illustrations on pages 10, 16, 23, 25, 26, 32, 63, 64, 70, 72, 73, and 78 are from *The Letters of Lewis Carroll,* edited by Morton N. Cohen, and are used by permission of Macmillan, London and Basingstoke.

Illustrations on pages 2, 5, 55, 66, 68, 69, 71, 82, 91, 101, and 103 courtesy of the Gernsheim Collection, Harry Ransom Humanities Research Center, The University of Texas at Austin.

Illustrations on pages 7, 8, 58, 61, 77, and 85 courtesy of the Photography Collection, Harry Ransom Humanities Research Center, The University of Texas at Austin.

First Edition   1   2   3   4   5   6   7   8   9   10

Library of Congress Cataloging in Publication Data

Bassett, Lisa.   Very truly yours, Charles L. Dodgson, alias Lewis Carroll.
Bibliography: p.   Summary: A biography, including excerpts from his letters, of the mathematician, teacher, photographer, and author who created "Alice in Wonderland" and many other stories. 1. Carroll, Lewis, 1832–1898—Biography—Juvenile literature. 2. Authors, English—19th century—Biography—Juvenile literature. [1. Carroll, Lewis, 1832–1898. 2. Authors, English] I. Title.
PR4612.B35   1987   828'.809 [B] [92]   85-10972   ISBN 0-688-06091-9

To
Jeni and Ralph
and Our Beloved "Drawling-Master"

Acknowledgments

I am indebted to Morton N. Cohen for his edition of *The Letters of Lewis Carroll* and to Roger L. Green for his edition of *The Diaries of Lewis Carroll*, and I offer my thanks to the Estate of C. L. Dodgson for their permission to publish selections from these volumes.

In the course of writing *Very Truly Yours, Charles L. Dodgson, Alias Lewis Carroll*, I received assistance, guidance, and support from numerous people. Although I am able to name only a few, my gratitude extends to all who have helped bring this book into existence. I wish to give special thanks to Edward Cohen of Rollins College, who encouraged me to begin researching and writing about Lewis Carroll and the "Alice" books; Maurice O'Sullivan of Rollins College; Elizabeth Butler-Cullingford of the University of Texas at Austin; the staff of the Harry Ransom Humanities Research Center at the University of Texas at Austin, especially Ken Craven, Patrice Fox, and Penny Moran; my editor, Dinah Stevenson; and Jerome Bump, for the manifold ways he has advanced my study of Alice and her creator.

Foreword

The unique power of this biography stems from Ms. Bassett's recognition that the most appropriate perspective for understanding Charles Dodgson is that of a child, because Dodgson's life was devoted to perpetuating childhood. As one of his child-friends put it, "He was one of us, and never a grown-up pretending to be a child in order to preach at us, or otherwise instruct us." Ms. Bassett focuses on Dodgson's own childhood; his meetings with children; the stories, poems, riddles, puns, drawings, photographs, lessons, and sermons he created for them; and finally his partings from them. Throughout, she shows us Dodgson's thoughts and feelings about these events and also, more rare in the scholarship, the perspectives and responses of his child-friends. The result is a significant contribution to our understanding not only of Charles Dodgson and Victorian literature, but of children's literature generally.

In this book we see Dodgson's interactions with children; more important, we experience them, from the children's point of view. The answers to riddles and puzzles are delayed to the end of the chapter, so that we may respond with pleasurable bafflement, as Dodgson's young friends did. In this and other ways, this biography invites the reader's participation. Deciphering the birthday picture-letter to Ina Watson, for instance, is a pleasant challenge to our creativity, particularly to our sense of humor.

Experiencing such a letter, and the personality of its author, from a child's point of view also helps us understand Dodgson's version of Christianity. The obvious text is, "'Let the children come to me . . . for it is to such as these that the kingdom of God belongs. I tell you solemnly, anyone who does not welcome the kingdom of God like a little child will never enter it'" (Mark 10:14–15). For Dodgson the essence of that kingdom was love, a key to stimulating creativity in others. Dodgson's success at communicating this shines through Ethel Rowell's memory of him: "'He gave me a sense of my own personal dignity. He was so punctilious, so courteous, so considerate, so scrupulous not to embarrass or offend, that he made me feel I counted'." In these pages, Ms. Bassett brings us the essential Dodgson.

Jerome Bump
Professor of English,
  University of Texas
Editor, *Texas Studies in Language
  and Literature*

Contents

Please observe this quite new
and original simile—treating friendship
as a clock! You see it needs the joining
of *two hands:* and though things
are sometimes at *sixes and sevens,*
yet they always *come round* at last.

C. L. Dodgson

in a letter to a child-friend,
February 1, 1891

"A Tale Begun in Other Days"

After *Alice's Adventures in Wonderland* was published in 1865, children were curious about the author. One child, Dolly Argles, wrote "Mr. Lewis Carroll" to ask him when he was going to write another book. Dolly received an answer, but it came from someone named Charles Lutwidge Dodgson:

> Dear Miss Dolly,
>   I have a message for you from a friend of mine, Mr. Lewis Carroll, who is a queer sort of creature, rather too fond of talking nonsense. He told me you had once asked him to write another book like one you had read—I forget the name—I think it was about "malice."
>   . . . If you have any message for him, you had better send it to
>
> Yours very truly,
Charles L. Dodgson

Dolly realized, of course, that Charles Dodgson and Lewis Carroll were *very* close friends—that, in fact, they were the same person. She wrote another letter and made this entry in her diary (where one can spell as one pleases): "Wrote to Mr. Dodson asked him what he was like."

Dolly again received an answer, but this one came from a fairy named Sylvie and was written in a miniature script. The letter read:

your loving friend
Charles L. Dodgson

Dear Lady,

Mr. Lewis Carroll asked me this morning if I would write to you instead of him, and give you some messages from him. First, he is much obliged to you for your nice letter, and he sends you a photograph of himself, so that you needn't wonder any more what he is like, and he hopes you will send him one of *yourself*. (He says I oughtn't to have put in that last bit: he meant the sentence to end at "is like.") . . .

I am your affectionate little fairy-friend,
Sylvie

A photograph of Lewis Carroll taken around 1872 shows what he looked like, but it does not tell what he was like, which is quite another matter. Dolly found out what sort of "creature" had two names and liked to talk nonsense because these letters marked the beginning of her friendship with Charles Dodgson. Many, many other children also discovered what he was like.

They found that knowing Charles Dodgson was something like meeting the characters from the Alice books. Sometimes he was as mild and sentimental as the White Knight, and sometimes he was as ridiculously cruel as the Duchess, who sings, "Speak roughly to your little boy, / And beat him when he sneezes." He could be as eager to quote poetry as Humpty Dumpty, but he could also be as anxious to teach lessons as the Mouse who gives a "dry" history lecture to the characters from the pool of tears. Often he was like Alice, who was "very fond of pretending to be two people." But Charles Dodgson was really only one person, a puzzling man, imaginative, eccentric, and perhaps best understood by the children he loved.

I. Childhood and Oxford

"It was much pleasanter at home," thought poor Alice. ". . . I almost wish I hadn't gone down that rabbit-hole—and yet—and yet—it's rather curious, you know, this sort of life! I do wonder what *can* have happened to me! When I used to read fairy tales, I fancied that kind of thing never happened, and now here I am in the middle of one! There ought to be a book written about me, that there ought!"

—*Alice's Adventures in Wonderland*

Charles Lutwidge Dodgson spent his earliest years in the midst of a steadily increasing number of sisters and brothers. Born on January 27, 1832, Charles was the first son, following two daughters, of the Reverend Charles Dodgson and Frances Jane Lutwidge Dodgson. Five sisters and three brothers were born after Charles, and thus the Dodgson children finally numbered eleven. Supporting the growing family, Charles's father, a clergyman in the Church of England, considered his earnings a "precarious income." But a photograph of the family's first home, the Parsonage of Daresbury, Cheshire, shows a comfortable, although unadorned, two-story

Very Truly Yours, Charles L. Dodgson, Alias Lewis Carroll

brick house surrounded by fields where the children must have played.

The Parsonage was on a secluded farm located a mile and a half from the village, and "even the passing of a cart was a matter of great interest to the children." Here Charles enjoyed the company of snails, toads, and earthworms, but rarely the company of children from outside the family. He played with his younger and older sisters and felt happy and at ease in this isolated household.

Naturally his sisters annoyed him at times, and at least once he found it necessary to protect his private property. On the back of a letter from his mother in which she had sent a million kisses to Charles and his sisters, he wrote: "No one is to touch this note, for it belongs to C.L.D." To be certain they would not touch it, he added: "Covered with slimy pitch, so they will wet their fingers." Even in this serious message, Charles shows his humor and imagination, two qualities that made him the leader of the family's games and amusements.

The Dodgsons moved from Daresbury when Charles was eleven years old and took up residence at the Rectory at Croft. Charles now was old enough to delight his family with his skillful handi-

Croft Rectory

work. He built a train out of "a wheelbarrow, a barrel and a small truck." The many paths in the kitchen garden served as railway tracks, and at various locations railway stations were set up to provide rest and refreshments for the passengers. Charles even wrote a list of rules for the game. The first rule declares that the "station master must mind his station, and supply refreshments: he can put anyone who behaves badly to prison, while a train goes round the garden." Another rule displays Charles's uncommon sense of humor: "All passengers when upset are requested to lie still until picked up—as it is requisite that at least 3 trains should go over them, to entitle them to the attention of the doctor and assistants."

Besides inventing the railway game, Charles also astounded his family with conjuring tricks, which he performed in the disguise of a brown wig and white robe. Charles loved drama and devised a puppet theater for his brothers and sisters. With the help of his family and the village carpenter, he made a troupe of marionettes and a stage. He wrote plays for the puppets and produced the shows, handling the complicated marionettes himself. During this time, Charles also wrote poetry, sketched, created stories, and edited family magazines full of amusing illustrations and poems.

These activities, however, were temporarily curtailed when Charles went to Richmond Grammar School at the age of twelve. His first encounter with the boys at school is described in a letter he wrote home, to his sisters Frances and Elizabeth and his brother Skeffington:

> Richmond School, Yorkshire
> August 5 [1844]

> The boys have played two tricks upon me which were these—they first proposed to play at "King of the cobblers" and asked me if I would be king, to which I agreed, then they made me sit down and sat (on the ground) in a circle round me, and told me to say "Go to work" which I said and they immediately began kicking me and knocking on all sides.

The second trick was also a "game," but the result was that Charles found his finger in the mouth of a strange boy who undoubtedly did not miss the opportunity of using his teeth. Later in the letter, Charles hints that he did not allow himself to be fooled without a fight, for he says simply, "The boys play me no tricks now."

For the most part, Charles enjoyed his time at this school, and he distinguished himself as a student. The headmaster, Mr. Tate, wrote a proud report to Charles's father: "I do not hesitate to express my opinion that he possesses, along with other and excellent natural endowments, a very uncommon share of genius."

After a year and a half, Charles left Richmond School, and his father sent him next to Rugby. Here he won many prizes for scholarship and again received much admiration and praise from his instructors, but he was not happy. Later in life, recalling his school days at Rugby, he wrote: "I cannot say that I look back upon my life at a Public School with any sensations of pleasure, or that any earthly considerations would induce me to go through my three years again." Although he made a few friends at Rugby, his relationships with the other boys were not entirely amiable. He did not participate in sports, preferring to spend his time studying and reading. In addition, he isolated himself because he was embarrassed by his stammer, an ailment that afflicted him all his life. The attitude of one other student toward the industrious, sensitive Charles was expressed in one of his schoolbooks, where he had signed his name. Following the signature, "C. L. Dodgson," come the cutting words, written in another handwriting, "is a muff." Returning home for vacations at Croft, where Charles was the beloved brother and praiseworthy son, must have been like returning to paradise.

Charles studied at Rugby for nearly four years and finally came

C. L. Dodgson, is a muff
School House,
Rugby,
Nov: 13. 1846.

home in 1849 to prepare for attending Oxford University. Again
he took charge of the Dodgson family entertainments. A new family magazine, *The Rectory Umbrella,* was a project from this period.
Charles wrote, illustrated, and edited the magazine. The fron-
tispiece of *The Rectory Umbrella* shows how an umbrella of jokes,
riddles, fun, poetry, and tales can act as a shield against boredom
and unhappiness. Charles believed in this same umbrella throughout his life and found that in creating fun for children, he made his
own protection from the unhappiness and loneliness that later
threatened him.

When Charles went into residence at Oxford University on January 24, 1851, his happy childhood came to a permanent close. He
had not only begun a new life in seriously intellectual surroundings, but on the second day after his arrival at Oxford, his mother
died. The joyous times at Croft had indeed come to an end, and
Charles Dodgson mourned for his mother as well as for the loss of
his childhood. At the age of twenty-one, two years after his
mother's death, he wrote a poem, "Solitude," that expresses his
emotional attachment to the past. The final stanza reads:

Very Truly Yours, Charles L. Dodgson, Alias Lewis Carroll

I'd give all wealth that years have piled,
The slow result of Life's decay,
To be once more a little child
For one bright summer-day.

Although a yearning for childhood ran strongly within Dodgson, he applied himself diligently to advancing in the adult world of Oxford. The university is divided into many colleges, and Dodgson studied at one of the most famous, Christ Church, a cathedral and college combined. As an undergraduate, Dodgson was awarded a Studentship of Christ Church which, like fellowships in other colleges and universities, provided him with an income that included benefits. Because Dodgson fulfilled the conditions of the Studentship by remaining unmarried and by progressing to Holy Orders, he received an income from the award for the rest of his life.

In 1854 he finished his undergraduate schooling, taking the degree of Bachelor of Arts. He continued to work toward his Master of Arts degree, which he received in 1857, and began to instruct private students in his rooms. A letter to his younger brother and sister describes the new experience:

My dear Henrietta,
My dear Edwin,
    . . . My one pupil has begun his work with me, and I will give you a description how the lecture is conducted. It is the most important point, you know, that the tutor should be *dignified,* and at a distance from the pupil, and that the pupil should be as much as possible *degraded*— otherwise you know, they are not humble enough. So I sit at the further end of the room; outside the door *(which is shut)* sits the scout; outside the outer door *(also shut)* sits the sub-scout; half-way down stairs sits the sub-sub-scout; and down in the yard sits the *pupil.*

    The questions are shouted from one to the other, and the answers come back in the same way—it is rather confusing till you are well used to it. The lecture goes on, something like this.

Tutor. "What is twice three?"

Scout. "What's a rice tree?"

Sub-Scout. "When is ice free?"

Sub-sub-Scout. "What's a nice fee?"

Pupil (timidly). "Half a guinea!"

Sub-sub-Scout. "Can't forge any!"

Sub-Scout. "Ho for jinny!"

Scout. "Don't be a ninny!"

Tutor (looks offended, but tries another question). . . .

In a much later letter to a child-friend, he drew a sketch to show how he looked when lecturing. His discomfort with his shyness and his stammer may account for the "expression of the brow" and "the action of the hand."

In the fall of 1855 Dodgson assumed the duties of a "Mathematical Lecturer," but despite his difficult schedule he managed to write and publish poetry and prose. Early in 1856 he sent "Solitude" to a new magazine, *The Train*. The editor accepted the poem for publication but requested that Dodgson use a pen name. By putting his second name before his first and using variations of Lutwidge and Charles (Lutwidge = Ludovicus = Lewis; Charles = Carolus = Carroll), Charles Lutwidge Dodgson created the name Lewis Carroll to sign to his writings. Both names belonged to a man who was as much a product of Oxford as of his golden childhood.

Oxford was Dodgson's home for forty-seven years, from his undergraduate days until his death, but he often sought release from the work and the somber surroundings of the College in his hobby of photography, in the pleasures of writing nonsense, and in the company of children. Looking back over his life, he wrote in 1896: "The friendship of children has always been a great element in my enjoyment of life, and is very *restful* as a contrast to the society of books, or of men."

II. Meetings

"You!" said the Caterpillar contemptuously. "Who are *you*?"

Which brought them back again to the beginning of the conversation. Alice felt a little irritated at the Caterpillar's making such *very* short remarks, and she drew herself up and said, very gravely, "I think you ought to tell me who *you* are, first."

—*Alice's Adventures in Wonderland*

Charles Dodgson met and made friends with children wherever he found them: in parks, at railway stations, on trains, in the homes of adult friends, at the seashore, or in Oxford. "[I] have more child-friends," he wrote, "than I could possibly count on my fingers, even if I were a centipede (by the way, *have* they fingers? . . .)." With his child-friends, Dodgson could be at ease; his stammer usually disappeared, and he could give his humor and playfulness free reign.

He did not, however, like all children. "Sometimes they are a real *terror* to me—" he explained in a letter, "especially boys: little girls I can now and then get on with, when they're few enough. . . . But with little *boys* I'm out of my element altogether." But children were only a *terror* "sometimes." Most often the girls, and occasionally a boy, quickly became friends with Mr. Dodgson. If he and the child got along during the first meeting, Dodgson soon began sending letters, gifts, and invitations. The children who received his notice had the opportunity to find out what Dodgson was like. Some of them formed friendships with him that lasted only a short time, while others gave him their affection until his death.

One child whom he met in Oxford became his favorite, his dream-child. Her name was Alice Liddell, and she would later be transformed into the imaginary Alice of *Alice's Adventures in Wonderland* and *Through the Looking-Glass.* When Dodgson first met Alice, however, he had no idea that she would one day inspire his greatest books of nonsense.

On the day of the meeting, Dodgson and an adult friend were experimenting with the new art of photography. They had taken a camera to the Deanery and were trying to photograph the Cathedral. The Deanery was the residence of the Reverend Henry George Liddell, Dean of Christ Church Cathedral and head of the College. His three little girls, Lorina, Alice, and Edith, were in the garden and must have been very curious about the two gentlemen with a camera. The date was April 25, 1856, and Dodgson wrote in his diary: "The three little girls were in the garden most of the time, and we became excellent friends: we tried to group them in the foreground of the picture, but they were not patient sitters." This chance meeting in the Deanery garden was only the first of many photography sessions for the children and the beginning of an important friendship between Dodgson and Alice. He marked the date in his diary as worthy of a "white stone," his way of designating special days.

Dodgson had a gift for easily making friends with children. He also recorded his first meeting with the children of George Mac-Donald, Mary and Greville. The meeting took place in the studio of an artist, where Greville was posing as the model for a sculpture. Dodgson wrote in his diary:

> They were a girl and boy, about seven and six years old—I claimed their acquaintance, and began at once proving to the boy, Greville, that he had better take the opportunity of having his head changed for a marble one. The effect was that in about two minutes they had entirely forgotten that I was a total stranger, and were earnestly arguing the question as if we were old acquaintances.

Dodgson suggested that a marble head would not have to be brushed and combed, and Greville almost agreed that such a head would be better than his own. But the debate continued and Greville finally realized that "a marble head couldn't speak," Dodgson wrote, "and as I couldn't convince either that he would be all the better for that, I gave in." Clearly, even an opening conversation with Dodgson might involve topics that grown-ups did not normally discuss.

Children recognized in Dodgson an adult who shared their interests and who spoke their favorite language of nonsense. They also found that he surrounded himself with a certain air of mysterious magic. Very often Dodgson would make friends with children on his travels. He would tell them stories or show them puzzles that he carried in a little black bag. After parting with his new friends and later arriving at his destination, Dodgson would send the children letters or gifts. Later in his life, the gifts were inscribed copies of *Alice's Adventures in Wonderland, Through the Looking-Glass,* or another of his books. In an accompanying letter he would reveal that he was not only Mr. Dodgson but also Lewis Carroll, the famous author, all mixed up in one person. Often the original meeting took place in only a matter of minutes, but the friendship that resulted could last for a lifetime.

Maud and Isabel Standen met Dodgson while he was waiting for a train. As always, he made friends with the children quickly, and when he returned home, he wrote a letter to Isabel that said:

> A friend of mine, called Mr. Lewis Carroll, tells me he means to send you a book. He is a *very* dear friend of mine. I have known him all my life (we are the same age) and have *never* left him. Of course he was with me in the Gardens, not a yard off—even while I was drawing those puzzles for you. I wonder if you saw him?
>
> Your fifteen-minute friend,
> C. L. Dodgson

Maud later remembered the occasion and wrote that the meeting was

> quite by accident, in the Forbury Gardens . . . He was waiting for a train to Oxford, and we went and sat on the same seat. He began to talk to us, and showed us puzzles and the tiniest of tiny scissors, which fascinated me, I remember, and which he kept in his pocket book. He made us write our names and address and then hurried off to catch his train. A day or two afterwards my sister received a copy of *Alice in Wonderland,* much to her delight. Soon after that he sent me *Through the Looking-Glass,* with a most delightful letter.

Another friend he acquired on a journey was Nellie Knight. She recalled that she first met Dodgson when he entered their carriage on the train. She remembered him as an "elderly gentleman, carrying a black bag." Dodgson brought from the bag pencils, notebooks, and puzzles to entertain Nellie and her brother until he had to change trains. Shortly after the meeting, Nellie received a copy of *Alice's Adventures Under Ground* in the mail, with a mysterious inscription on the flyleaf. None of the Knight family could discover what the strange writing meant. Finally they found that the words could be read if the page was held up to a mirror:

> Nellie Knight
> A Souvenir of a
> puzzling Railway-journey
> taken Aug. 20, 1888
> From the Author

The book was followed by a formal letter:

> Care of Messrs. Macmillan
> 29 Bedford Street, Covent Garden, London
> August 28, 1888

> Mr. Lewis Carroll presents his respectful compliments to Miss Nellie Knight, and would be glad to know whether she received a little book which he sent for her acceptance on the 21st of this month, and if it is her gracious pleasure to keep it, or if she despises it so much that she would prefer to return it. If she decides to keep it he would be glad, in order to prevent jealousy, to send a book for the little boy—some distant relation of hers, he thinks—who was travelling with her.

Another letter in Dodgson's usual teasing tone arrived a few days later. Nellie remembered the first meeting clearly, and declared that during the conversation she never said "shan't" and "won't."

> 7 Lushington Road, Eastbourne
> September 1, 1888

My dear Nellie,

One grand letter is enough. I'm going to sign my real name to this. The other one I use for my books, because

I don't want to be known, except by *friends*. Now it seemed to me that you and I *had* to be *friends*. Even when I got into the carriage and said "Now *please* don't get up on *my* account, do lie down again!" and you said "Shan't! You mind your own business!" I only thought "Oh, well, we shall do better soon!" And even when I offered you a puzzle to try and you said "*Won't!* Don't care for puzzles!" still I thought "Oh, something must have put her out of temper. It won't last long!" The most discouraging time, I think, was when I said "Do look here, Nellie! Sydney has found out this puzzle!" and you said "*Hasn't!* He never found out a puzzle in all his life!" I *almost* gave up hope then. However, I thought "I'll *send* her something—either a Chelsea Bun, or a book! And then, perhaps, she won't be quite so cross!" It took me three or four months to settle *which* to send you. I wonder if I chose right? Would you rather have a Chelsea Bun?

I'm rather puzzled which book to send to Sydney. He looks so young for *Through the Looking-Glass*. However, he found out one puzzle . . . that I don't remember any one of his age ever guessing before: so I think it won't be too old a book for him.

I wish you didn't live so far off. I'm afraid we shall never meet again. Why don't you come and stay at Eastbourne a little? It's a charming place, and I hope to be here till about the 10th of October. My real home is "Christ Church, Oxford": but I come here every summer.

Your new, old ("new" as a friend, "old" as a human being), affectionate friend,

Charles L. Dodgson

Dodgson spent his summers at the seaside, and Sandown and

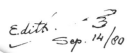

Dodgson's sketch of Edith Blakemore
at Eastbourne

Eastbourne were two of his favorite places to vacation. The beaches were alive with children, giving Dodgson many opportunities to make new friends. May Mileham became one of his friends at Eastbourne, and her cousin later described May's first meeting with Dodgson:

> On one of our low-tide explorations of the chalk-rock pools . . . [May] slipped and fell full-length in a few inches of water. Refusing to see the funny side of the incident and regarding with dismay her sodden garments, she set up a piercing howl. . . . From the distant crowded parade emerged a black-coated figure of clerical aspect, striding in haste over shingle and sand-flat. Gathering up in his arms the wet mess of my amphibious cousin, he bore her with soothing words to the lodgings. . . . It was somehow borne in upon me that I was probably the cause of the trouble, and that, anyhow, little boys were of no account, unless conceivably the getting in a mess and making an inordinate fuss should render them of interest to the gentleman who I now learned was the author of *Alice in Wonderland*.

Another friend, Gertrude Chataway, was intensely curious about Dodgson before she met him. She wrote of the experience:

> Imagine the sea-side at Sandown . . . where lodgings stretched along the front each with its balcony on the upper floor and standing in a little garden with steps leading down on to the shore. Imagine a little girl of about 8½ absolutely entranced with the lodger next door. To her he seemed quite an old gentleman. In the morning he came out on to his balcony breathing in the sea air as if he would not get enough; and whenever she heard him coming she would rush out on to the balcony

to see him. After a few days he spoke to her: "Little girl why do you come so fast on to your balcony whenever I come out?" "To see you sniff," she said. "It is lovely to see you sniff like this"—she threw up her head and drew in the air. Thus began a long friendship which ended only with his death.

One of Dodgson's correspondents, a man named Bowles, had a young daughter, Sydney, about whom he must have written to Dodgson. A month before he actually met Sydney, Dodgson wrote her a letter, which expresses something of his delight in the discovery of a new child-friend and his enjoyment of the unrestrained affection that children so readily gave him:

> Christ Church, Oxford
> May 22, 1891

My *dear* Sydney,

I *am* so sorry, and so ashamed! Do you know, I didn't even know of your *existence*? And it was *such* a surprise to hear that you had sent me your love! It felt just as if Nobody had suddenly run into the room, and had given me a kiss! (That's a thing which happens to me, *most* days, just now.) If only I had known you were existing, I would have sent you *heaps* of love, long ago. And, now I come to think about it, I ought to have sent you the love, without being so particular about whether you existed or not. In *some* ways, you know, people that *don't* exist, are much nicer than people that *do*. For instance, people that *don't* exist are never *cross*: and they never *contradict* you: and *they never tread on your toes!* Oh, they're *ever* so much nicer than people that *do* exist! However, never mind: you can't help existing, you know; and I daresay you're *just* as nice as if you didn't.

Which of my books shall I give you, now that I know

you're a real child? Would you like *Alice in Wonderland*? Or *Alice Under Ground*? (That's the book just as I first wrote it, with my own pictures.)

Please give my love, and a kiss, to Weenie, and Vera, and yourself (don't forget the *kiss* to yourself, please: on the forehead is the best place).

> Your affectionate friend,
> Lewis Carroll

Meeting Dodgson for the first time was exciting, memorable, and often puzzling. Children shortly discovered that they had found a new friend, but precisely *who* the interesting gentleman was remained a mystery. Was he Lewis Carroll or Mr. Charles L. Dodgson or both? Dodgson himself realized that a first meeting could present some complexities, and his letter to Magdalen Millard shows just how confusing an encounter with the author of *Alice in Wonderland* could be.

> Christ Church, Oxford
> December 15, 1875

My dear Magdalen,

I want to explain to you why I did not call yesterday. I was sorry to miss you, but you see I had so many conversations on the way. I tried to explain to the people in the street that I was going to see you, but they wouldn't listen; they said they were in a hurry, which was rude. At last I met a wheelbarrow that I thought would attend to me, but I couldn't make out what was in it. I saw some features at first, then I looked through a telescope, and found it was a countenance; then I looked through a microscope, and found it was a face! I thought it was rather like me, so I fetched a large looking-glass to make sure, and then to my great joy I found it was me. We shook hands, and were just beginning to talk, when myself came up and joined us, and we had quite a pleasant conversation. I said, "Do you remember when we all met at Sandown?" and myself said, "It was very jolly there; there was a child called Magdalen," and me said, "I used to like her a little; not much, you know—only a little." Then it was time for us to go to the train, and who do you think came to the station to see us off? You would never guess, so I must tell you. They were two very dear friends of mine, who happen to be here just now, and beg to be allowed to sign this letter, as

Your affectionate friends,
Lewis Carroll, and C. L. Dodgson

III. Letters

"There's more evidence to come yet, please your Majesty," said the White Rabbit, jumping up in a great hurry: "this paper has just been picked up."

"What's in it?" said the Queen.

"I haven't opened it yet," said the White Rabbit; "but it seems to be a letter, written by the prisoner to—to somebody."

"It must have been that," said the King, "unless it was written to nobody, which isn't usual, you know."

—*Alice's Adventures in Wonderland*

After the initial meeting with a child, Dodgson encouraged a lively and imaginative correspondence. Many letters would fly back and forth between himself and his new friend. The children eagerly awaited Dodgson's letters, which were filled with nonsense, stories, poems, and drawings. Writing to children gave Dodgson a freedom of expression that his life at Oxford often suppressed. He could tease and joke and puzzle his young readers without restraint. But occasionally he found it necessary to remind children that his letters should only bring laughter. He wrote to Agnes Hull in a rather serious tone, warning against taking his words for anything but nonsense:

Christ Church, Oxford
December 18, 1879

My darling Aggie,

. . . Really you mustn't begin to believe my letters to be all meant seriously, or I shall be so frightened I shan't dare to write to you . . . I was only talking nonsense. It's a way I have.

And so you think we're going to meet *soon*? And that there isn't time for many more letters? Now to *me* it seems, oh such a long way off! Hours and hours: 30 or 40 at least. And I should say there is plenty of time for *fifteen* more letters—4 today, 8 tomorrow, and 3 on Saturday morning. You'll get so used to hearing the postman's knock, that at last you'll only say, "Oh, another letter from Mr. Dodgson, of course!" and when the maid brings it in, you'll only say, "Haven't time to read it: put it in the fire!" . . .

But I must leave off *this* letter, or I shan't have comfortable time for my other 4 letters to you today.

Your loving friend,
C.L.D.

Dodgson knew exactly what sort of letters his friends would enjoy receiving. Once he advised Mary MacDonald of the correct way to write a letter:

Now I want to know what you *mean* by calling yourself "naughty" for not having written sooner! Naughty, indeed! Stuff and nonsense! Do you think *I'd* call myself naughty, if I hadn't written to you, say for 50 years? Not a bit! I'd just begin as usual "My dear Mary, 50 years ago, you asked me what to do for your kitten, as it had a tooth-ache, and I have just remembered to write about it. Perhaps the tooth-ache has gone off by this time—if not, wash it carefully in hasty-pudding, and give it 4 pincushions boiled in sealing-wax, and just dip the end of its tail in hot coffee. This remedy has never been known to fail." There! *That's* the proper way to write!

At times Dodgson's letters took extraordinary forms. A letter to Dymphna Ellis, for instance, was probably written with a fine geographer's pen, and reading the tiny "fairy" script requires a magnifying glass:

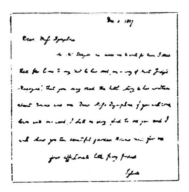

Dec 2, 1867

Dear Miss Dymphna,

As Mr. Dodgson has asked me to write for him, I send these few lines to say that he has sent you a copy of *Aunt Judy's Magazine*: that you may read the little story he has written about Bruno and me. Dear Miss Dymphna, if you will come down into our wood, I shall be very glad to see you and I will show you the beautiful garden Bruno made for me.

Your affectionate little fairy friend,
Sylvie

A letter to Nelly Bowman begins at the end and ends at the beginning:

Nov. 1. 1891.

C.L.D., Uncle loving your! Instead grandson his to it give to had you that so, years 80 or 70 for it forgot you that was it pity a what and: him of fond so were you wonder don't I and, gentleman old nice very a was he. For it made you that *him* been have *must* it see you so: *grandfather* my was, *then* alive was that, "Dodgson Uncle" only the. Born was *I* before long was that, see you, then But. "Dodgson Uncle for pretty thing some make I'll now", it began you when, yourself to said you that, me telling her without, knew I course of and: ago years many great a it made had you said she. Me told Isa what from was it? For meant was it who out made I how know you do! Lasted has it well how and. Grandfather my for made had you Antimacassar pretty that me give to you of nice so was it, Nelly dear my.

Other letters could only be read with a looking glass, such as this note to Margaret (Daisy) Brough. When viewed in a mirror it reads:

Ch[rist] Ch[urch]
Oxford
Nov. 24/83

My dear Daisy,
    I enclose you the Rules for that game I taught you. Also the puzzle of "Doublets" for your sister. I was very nearly writing on it "for Polly", when luckily I remembered that she is probably *very* old, & would be *very*

Very Truly Yours, Charles L. Dodgson, Alias Lewis Carroll

much offended. Would you give me a list of your names, ages, & birthdays?

> Yours affectionately,
> Lewis Carroll.

In Dodgson's handwriting the note looks like this:

Dodgson rarely gave birthday presents, but he often sent special birthday letters. Here is one to Ina Watson:

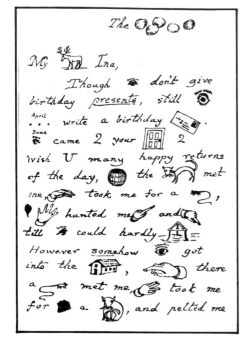
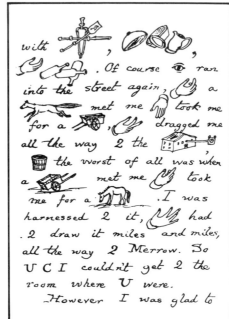

A translation of the birthday picture-letter:

                                        The Chestnuts

My dear Ina,

    Though I don't give birthday *presents*, still I may write a birthday letter. I came to your door to wish you many happy returns of the day, but the cat met me, and took me for a mouse, and hunted me up and down till I could hardly stand. However *some*how I got into the house, and there a mouse met me, and took me for a cat, and pelted me with fire irons, crockery, and bottles. Of course I ran into the street again, and a horse met me and took me for a cart, and dragged me all the way to the Guildhall, but the worst of all was when a cart met me and took me for a horse. I was harnessed to it, and had to draw it miles and miles, all the way to Merrow. So you see I couldn't get to the room where you were.

Very Truly Yours, Charles L. Dodgson, Alias Lewis Carroll

However I was glad to hear you were hard at work learning the multiplication tables for a birthday treat.

I had just time to look into the kitchen, and saw your birthday feast getting ready, a nice dish of crusts, bones, pills, cotton-bobbins, and rhubarb and magnesia. "Now," I thought, "she will be happy!" and with a smile I went on my way.

Your affectionate friend,
C.L.D.

At times, Dodgson wrote letters about the difficulties of writing. Adelaide Paine received a letter that said:

Christ Church, Oxford
March 8, 1880

My dear Ada,

(Isn't that your short name? "Adelaide" is all very well, but you see when one is *dreadfully* busy one hasn't time to write such long words—particularly when it takes one half an hour to remember how to spell it—and even then one has to go and get a dictionary to see if one has spelt it right, and of course the dictionary is in another room, at the top of a high bookcase—where it has been for months and months, and has got all covered with dust—so one has to get a duster first of all, and nearly choke oneself in dusting it—and when one *has* made out at last which is dictionary and which is dust, even *then* there's the job of remembering which end of the alphabet "A" comes—for one feels pretty certain it isn't in the *middle*—then one has to go and wash one's hands before turning over the leaves—for they've got so thick with dust one hardly knows them by sight—and, as likely as not, the soap is lost, and the jug is empty, and there's no towel, and one has to spend hours and hours in finding things—and perhaps after all one has to go off to the shop to buy a new cake of soap—so, with all this bother, I hope you won't mind my writing it short and saying, "My dear Ada.") . . .

Your very affectionate friend,
Lewis Carroll

And another problem arose in writing to a boy named Bert Coote.

The Chestnuts, Guildford
June 9 [?1877]

My dear Bertie,

I would have been very glad to write to you as you wish, only there are several objections. I think, when you have heard them, you will see that I am right in saying "No."

The first objection is, I've got no ink. You don't believe it? Ah, you should have seen the ink there was in *my* days! (About the time of the battle of Waterloo: I was a soldier in that battle.) Why, you had only to pour a little of it on the paper, and it went on by itself! *This* ink is so stupid, if you begin a word for it, it can't even finish it by itself.

The next objection is, I've no time. You don't believe *that*, you say? Well, who cares? You should have seen the time there was in *my* days! (At the time of the battle of Waterloo, where I led a regiment.) There were always 25 hours in the day—sometimes 30 or 40.

The third and greatest objection is, my *great* dislike for children. I don't know why, I'm sure: but I *hate* them—just as one hates armchairs and plum-pudding! You don't believe *that*, don't you? Did I ever say you would? Ah, you should have seen the children there were in *my* days! (Battle of Waterloo, where I commanded the English army. I was called "the Duke of

Wellington" then, but I found it a great bother having such a long name, so I changed it to "Mr. Dodgson." I chose that name because it begins with the same letter as "Duke.") So you see it would never do to write to you.

Have you any sisters? I forget. If you have, give them my love. . . .

I hope you won't be much disappointed at not getting a letter from

Your affectionate friend,
C. L. Dodgson

Certainly Dodgson was a busy man, and at least once he wrote a rather short "long" letter:

Christ Church, Oxford
May 22, 1887

My dear Winnie,

But you will be getting tired of this long letter: so I will bring it to an end, and sign myself

Yours affectionately,
C. L. Dodgson

At times his friends had to do what the White Queen in *Through the Looking-Glass* boasts of when she says, "I can read words of one letter! Isn't *that* grand?"

My dear Annie,

A picture, which I hope will

B one that you will like to

C. If your Mamma should

D sire one like it, I could

E sily get her one.

Your affectionate friend,
C. L. Dodgson

Violet Dodgson, his niece, might have read this letter without realizing there was anything unusual about it:

Christ Church, Oxford
May 6, 1889

Dear Violet,

I'm glad to hear you children like the Magazine I ordered for you for a year: and if you happen to have seen the book about "Lord Fauntleroy," you'll find an interesting bit about the child that acts the Boy (now they have made a Play of it) in Number Six. She seems to be a child without one bit of pride: a pretty name too, hasn't she? the little "Elsie Leslie Lyde." I grieve to hear your bantam-hen is fond of rolling eggs away. You should remind it, now and then, of "Waste not, want not." You should say "a bantam-hen, that wastes an egg, is sure to get extremely poor, and to be forced at last to beg for hard-boiled eggs, from door to door. How would you like it, Bantam-hen," you should go on, "if all your brood were hard-boiled chickens? You would then be sorry you had been so rude!" Tell it all this, and don't forget! And now I think it's time for me to sign myself, dear Violet,

Your loving Uncle,
C.L.D.

Here is another way to read Violet's letter:

> Dear Violet, I'm glad to hear
> you children like the Magazine
> I ordered for you for a year:
> and if you happen to have seen
> the book about "Lord Fauntleroy,"
> you'll find an interesting bit
> about the child that acts the Boy
> (now they have made a Play of it)

in Number Six. She seems to be
a child without one bit of pride:
a pretty name too, hasn't she?
the little "Elsie Leslie Lyde."
I grieve to hear your bantam-hen
is fond of rolling eggs away.
You should remind it, now and then,
of "Waste not, want not." You should say
"a bantam-hen, that wastes an egg,
is sure to get extremely poor,
and to be forced at last to beg
for hard-boiled eggs, from door to door.
How would you like it, Bantam-hen,"
you should go on, "if all your brood
were hard-boiled chickens? You would then
be sorry you had been so rude!"
Tell it all this, and don't forget!
And now I think it's time for me
to sign myself, dear Violet,
Your loving Uncle, C.L.D.

Agnes Hull was fortunate enough to receive a little notebook that Dodgson had made for her. It contained poems and riddles devised especially for her. After seeing the notebook, Agnes returned it to Dodgson with the hope that he would add more of his writings to the pages. But Dodgson wrote an alarming letter upon receiving the notebook by book-post:

Christ Church, Oxford
October 17, 1878

WELL! of all the *mean* things ever done by a young lady of ten to save *one penny*, I think the sending that *precious* little book, on which I have spent so many *sleepless* hours, by book-post, so as to make sure that all its corners should get well bruised on the way, and the book itself should be read all through by the post-office clerks (who always read such books just after putting coals on the fire, so as to leave black thumb-marks all through it), and that the beautiful leather cover should be scratched by the post-office cats—was about the *meanest*! You hardly deserve to have it back again, you dreadful child! Of course I know your *real* motive—that you thought, if you sent it by post, I should expect you to write a note with it, and you were too proud to do *that*! Oh, this pride, this pride! How it spoils a child who would otherwise be quite endurable! And pride of birth is the worst of all. Besides, *I* don't believe the Hull family is as old as you say: it's all nonsense that idea of yours, that Japhet took the surname Hull because he was the one that built the hull of the Ark. I'm not at all sure that it *had* a hull. And when you say his wife was called Agnes, and that you are named after her, you know you're simply inventing. And anyhow, *I'm* descended from Japhet too: so you needn't turn up your nose (and chin, and eyes, and hair) so *very* high! . . .

Your loving friend,
Lewis Carroll

And another letter on the same subject gets revenge on the frugal Agnes in an interesting manner:

> Why, how can she know that no harm has
> gazing at it for hours together with
> for instance, the number of beetles
> myself "your loving" you g...
> then I go down another
> truly, Lewis Carroll.
> Oct. 22/78

The letter to Agnes Hull is translated:

> Why, how *can* she know that no harm has come to it? Surely *I* must know best, having the book before me from morning to night, and gazing at it *for hours together* with tear-dimmed eyes? Why, there were several things I didn't even mention, for instance, the number of beetles that had got crushed between the leaves. So when *I* sign myself "your loving" *you* go down a step, & say "your affectionate"? Very well, then *I* go down *another* step, & sign myself "yours truly, 'Lewis Carroll.'"
>
> Oct. 22/78

But this was not the end of the notebook. Another letter to Agnes, who refused to "rise" for early morning walks, followed:

> Christ Church, Oxford
> November 16, 1878
>
> My dear Agnes,
>
> . . . As to your book, don't you know what a useful virtue *patience* is? You had better add it to the painfully small stock of virtues you have got at present. (Your character, *at present*, being made up of two things only—deceit and sulkiness, with perhaps a *few* grains of greediness.) The book is really so disfigured with dead beetles, I can't possibly send it till it has been to the laundress (and I haven't yet found one who can wash it: it wants a laundress who can "get up" *book*-muslin). Besides, I've only invented one new conundrum: "Why is Agnes like a thermometer?" "Because she won't *rise* when it's cold" and perhaps you wouldn't like *that* put in. . . . Send the crippled boy's name and address, and I'll send him an *Easter Greeting.*
>
> Your loving friend,
> C. L. Dodgson

As the conclusion of the last letter suggests, Dodgson could switch suddenly from a joking tone to one of seriousness. Underlying all his fun and teasing existed a sincere desire for the trust, respect, and affection of his child-friends. In a letter to Edith Rix, he wrote:

My dear Child,

. . . And now I come to the most interesting part of your letter—May you treat me as a perfect friend, and write anything you like to me, and ask my advice? Why, *of course* you may, my child! What else am I good for? But oh, my dear child-friend, you cannot guess how such words sound to *me*! That any one should look up to *me*, or think of asking *my* advice—well, it makes one feel humble, I think, rather than proud—humble to remember, while others think so well of me, what I really *am*, in myself. "Thou, that teachest another, teachest thou not thyself?" Well, I won't talk about myself, it is not a healthy topic. Perhaps it may be true of *any* two people, that, if one could see the other through and through, love would perish. I don't know. Anyhow, I like to *have* the love of my child-friends, though I know I don't deserve it. Please write as freely as *ever* you like. . . .

IV. Invitations and Visits

The Fish-Footman began by producing from under his arm a great letter, nearly as large as himself, and this he handed over to the other, saying, in a solemn tone, "For the Duchess. An invitation from the Queen to play croquet." The Frog-Footman repeated, in the same solemn tone, . . . "From the Queen. An invitation for the Duchess to play croquet."

Then they both bowed low, and their curls got entangled together.

Alice laughed so much at this, that she had to run back into the wood for fear of their hearing her. . . .

—*Alice's Adventures in Wonderland*

As a friendship between Dodgson and a child developed, his letters often contained invitations. A child-friend might be asked to join him for any number of activities, ranging from a walk and tea in his rooms to an excursion in London to attend plays, concerts, museums, picture galleries, or pantomimes. Usually the child-visitor came with a governess or with family members. But Dodgson liked to get to know children individually, and he preferred being entrusted with them one at a time.

To invite Enid Stevens, Dodgson wrote to her mother:

When do you think [Enid] will have the courage to come *alone* with me, for a walk and tea? I observed one favourable sign, for her soon feeling at home with me—that she didn't, as so many children do when brought by mothers, leave it *wholly* to the mother to talk, but had a tongue of her own.

Apparently Enid felt quite "at home" with Dodgson and wrote to tell him that she would be glad to come for a walk and tea. Dodgson, thrilled, wrote to explain his new plans for the visit:

Christ Church, Oxford
April 7, 1891

My DEAR Enid,

So you think you've got the courage to come a walk by yourself with me? Indeed! Well, I shall come for you on April 31st at 13 o'clock, and first I will take you to the Oxford Zoological Gardens, and put you into a cage of LIONS, and when they've had a good feed, I'll put whatever is left of you into a cage of TIGERS. Then I'll bring you to my rooms, and give a regular beating, with a thick stick, to my new little friend. Then I'll put you into the coal-hole, and feed you for a week on nothing but bread and water. Then I'll send you home in a milk-cart, in one of the empty milk-cans. And after that, if ever I come for you again, you'll scream louder than a COCKATOO!

Your loving friend,
Lewis Carroll

In a letter to Beatrice Earle, Dodgson reveals how skillfully he was able to turn anxieties into a laughing matter.

The shaky letter is translated:

Ch. Ch.
Feb. 3/84

My dear B,

  You were so gracious the other day that I have nearly
got over my fear of you. The slight tremulousness,
which you may observe in my writing, produced by the
thought that it is *you* I am writing to, will soon pass off.
Next time I borrow you, I shall venture on having you
alone: I like my child-friends best *one by one:* & I'll have
Maggie alone another day *if she'll come* (*that* is the *great*
difficulty!). But first I want to borrow (I can *scarcely*
muster courage to say it!) your *eldest* sister. Oh, how the

very thought of it frightens me! Do you think she would come? I don't mean alone: I think Maggie might come too, to make it all proper.

When all fears were overcome and the actual visit took place, the experience gained a permanent place in the child's memories. Another of Dodgson's friends, Ethel Arnold, remembered what a visit to his rooms was like:

> What an El Dorado of delights those rooms were to his innumerable child friends! The large sitting room was lined with well-filled bookshelves, under which ran a row of cupboards all round the four walls. Oh, those cupboards! What wondrous treasures they contained for the delectation of youth! Mechanical bears, dancing dolls, toys and puzzles of every description, came from them in endless profusion. Even after I was grown up I never paid a visit to his rooms without experiencing over again a thrill of delicious anticipation when a cupboard door swung open.

Besides the toys and puzzles, Dodgson also had an "orguinette" that played music from paper sheets and had to be turned by hand. In addition, there were "some fourteen or more musical-boxes," Evelyn Hatch recalled, "which entranced the listener with their tinkling, fairy-like tunes."

Edith Alice Litton loved to join her father when he visited Dodgson. In his rooms, Edith wrote, she enjoyed "delicious slices of cake and bread-and-butter, the glass of creamy milk; the soft pile of cushions on the sofa if I felt tired, and . . . the lovely picture-books which I was so careful not to tear." Visits with Dodgson gave Edith an education that she never forgot. She wrote:

> I always attribute my love for animals to the teaching of Mr. Dodgson: his stories about them, his knowledge of

their lives and histories, his enthusiasm about birds and butterflies enlivened many a dull hour. The monkeys in the Botanical Gardens were our special pets, and when we fed them with nuts and biscuits he seemed to enjoy the fun as much as I did.

But if Dodgson sometimes acted as a teacher on these excursions, he knew what type of lessons a child would enjoy most. Gertrude Chataway received this invitation:

> Christ Church, Oxford
> February 11, 1877

My dearest Gertrude,

Is there any chance of your being in London in the course of the next 4 weeks? I *should* so like to take you to see *Goody Two Shoes*, the Pantomime at the Adelphi Theatre. It is all acted by children (there are nearly 100 in it) and two of them, the little Clown and Columbine, are friends of mine, and very nice children they are— and wonderfully clever. I wonder if you have ever seen a Pantomime at all? If not, your education is *quite* incomplete, and you had better tell your parents that they mustn't put your lessons in the wrong order! The next lesson ought to be "Pantomime"; then "French"; then "German"; and so on. It never does to begin education at the end, and work back: that will only confuse your poor brain. From

> Your loving friend,
> Lewis Carroll

Dodgson had already been to see *Goody Two Shoes* and had recorded his admiration for two of the child performers in his diary: "Little Bertie Coote (about 10) was Clown—a wonderfully clever little fellow: and Carrie (about 8) was Columbine, a very pretty graceful little thing—in a few years time she will be just *the* child to act 'Alice', if it is ever dramatised." At that time, Dodgson had gone backstage after the performance and had begun what would become a friendship with the Coote family. Bert Coote remembered how

> Mr. Dodgson often came behind the scenes, and all the children in the show adored him. I well remember my sisters, Carrie and Lizzie, and I spending a day with him at Oxford and being vastly entertained by his collection of elaborate mechanical toys. The autographed copies of his books and photographs which he gave me are among my most cherished possessions. . . . We never gave imitations of Lewis Carroll, or shared any joke in which he could not join—he was one of us, and never a grown-up pretending to be a child in order to preach at us, or otherwise instruct us. . . . I shall never forget the morning he took my sister and I over the Tower of London and how fascinated we were by the stories he told us about it and its famous prisoners. I suspect now that very few of them were based on strict, historical fact, but that they would have charmed any child there is no question.

Another boy, Greville MacDonald, vividly recalled how "Uncle Dodgson" would take the children to the Polytechnic "to see the 'dissolving views' of Christmas Fairy Tales." And that there was "a toy-shop in Regent Street where he let us choose gifts, one of which will remain my own as long as memory endures. It was an unpainted, wooden horse. I loved it as much as any girl her doll." But all boys were not treated so affectionately. Mrs. Alice Collett remembered a time when

> kind "Lewis Carroll" took me on his knee and told me stories and drew pictures for me. I had the luck to be

called Alice and to have a quantity of fair hair, so he took a fancy to me, while my poor brother, who knew "Alice" almost by heart, gazed at its author with adoring eyes but had no notice taken of him.

Later in his life, Dodgson began inviting girls not just for tea or dinner but for longer visits of several days or more. When Ruth Gamlen was a child of ten, Dodgson invited her to visit him at Eastbourne. She recalled the plans for the trip:

> He would arrange for me to stay in the house of three old ladies, friends of his, and he would look after me in the day time. My parents were quite firm in not allowing me to go away with him, and I was not at all disappointed. The old ladies sounded formidable, and tho' I liked Mr. Dodgson very much I did not want to be with him all day long.

Enid Stevens had very different feelings about an invitation from Dodgson. She wrote:

> Over and over again he begged my mother to let him take me away with him—sometimes to the seaside, sometimes to London. The Victorian mind saw possible evil in the association of a child of twelve with an old man of sixty-three. He must have had wonderful patience, for he tried again and again, but I was never allowed to go and shall never to the end of my days cease to regret it.

Gossip about Dodgson and the girl guests who were allowed to stay with him must have circulated widely, for rumors reached his family. Dodgson answered a concerned letter from his sister with firm disregard for the criticism leveled against him:

7 Lushington Road, Eastbourne
September 21, 1893

My dearest Mary,

. . . I *do* like getting such letters as yours. I think all you say about my girl guests is most kind and sisterly, and most entirely proper for you to write to your brother. But I don't think it at all advisable to enter into any controversy about it. There is no reasonable probability that it would modify the views either of you or of me. I will say a few words to explain my views: but I have no wish whatever to have "the last word": so please say anything you like afterwards.

You and your husband have, I think, been very fortunate to know so little, by experience, in your own case or in that of your friends, of the wicked recklessness with which people repeat things to the disadvantage of others, without a thought as to whether they have grounds for asserting what they say. I have met with a good deal of utter misrepresentation of that kind. And another result of my experience is the conviction that the opinion of "people" in general is absolutely worthless as a test of right and wrong. The only two tests I now apply to such a question as the having some particular girl-friend as a guest are, first, my own *conscience*, to settle whether I feel it to be entirely innocent and right, in the sight of God; secondly, the *parents* of my friend, to settle whether I have their *full* approval for what I do. You need not be shocked at my being spoken against. *Any-body*, who is spoken about at all, is *sure* to be spoken against by *somebody:* and any action, however innocent in itself, is liable, and not at all unlikely, to be blamed by *somebody.* If you limit your actions in life to things that *nobody* can possibly find fault with, you will not do much!

Despite Dodgson's apparent indifference to being talked about, he was always careful to observe Victorian propriety. One child-friend, Ruth Gamlen, recalled what happened when Isa Bowman came to visit him at Oxford: "In order that there should be no ill-natured gossip about her visit he arranged for her to stay in the house of an old lady who, my mother said, was gossip's very fountainhead, so associating her with Isa's visit and stopping all chatter at its source."

Isa Bowman, a child actress who played Alice in a stage production of *Alice in Wonderland,* was one of Dodgson's favorite friends. He wrote a journal for her, describing her stay in Oxford. The visit began, according to Dodgson, like this:

Isa's Visit to Oxford, 1888

Chapter I

On Wednesday, the Eleventh of July, Isa happened to meet a friend at Paddington Station at half-past ten. She can't remember his name, but she says he was an old old old gentleman, and he had invited her, she thinks, to go with him somewhere or other, she can't remember where.

Other excerpts from the journal give an idea of how Dodgson's guests spent their time. Dodgson refers to himself as the "Aged Aged Man," or "A.A.M."

They had breakfast at Ch[rist] Ch[urch], in the rooms of the A.A.M., and then Isa learned how to print with the "Type-Writer," and printed several beautiful volumes of poetry, all of her own invention.

And on another day:

Isa had a Music Lesson, and learned to play on an

American Orguinette. It is not a *very* difficult instrument to play, as you only have to turn a handle round and round: so she did it nicely. You put a long piece of paper in, and it goes through the machine, and the holes in the paper make different notes play. They put one in wrong end first, and had a tune backwards, and soon found themselves in the day before yesterday. So they dared not go on, for fear of making Isa so young she would not be able to talk.

During the last night

she went to bed, and dreamed she was fixed in the middle of Oxford, with her feet fast to the ground, and her head between the bars of a cellar window, in a sort of final tableau. Then she dreamed the curtain came down, and the people all called out "encore!" But she cried out, "Oh, not again! It would be *too* dreadful to have my visit all over again!" But, on second thoughts, she smiled in her sleep, and said, "Well, do you know, after all I think I wouldn't mind so very much if I *did* have it all over again!"

Isa and many other girls were allowed to visit Dodgson for vacations at the seaside. Violet Dodgson remembered her visit and wrote:

At the age of about thirteen, I was honoured but slightly alarmed by an invitation to spend ten days with him in his rooms at Eastbourne—ten days so crowded with good things that I had no time to feel lost or homesick (as one usually did when separated from one's family). We did "lessons" in the morning. . . . The rest of the day went on a variety of amusements, expeditions to here, there, and everywhere, concerts, theatres (five plays

Very Truly Yours, Charles L. Dodgson, Alias Lewis Carroll

in the ten days), talks on the beach, every day ending with games of backgammon, &c., which removed my bed-time almost into the small hours and sent me home finally a somewhat washed-out little person. I probably bored him: he liked children to talk and we were rather dumb. But he never let me see it and was the most thoughtful, courteous, and unwearying of hosts.

Dodgson's account of a visit from Phoebe Carlo at Eastbourne reveals that sometimes he did feel the gap that existed between his young friends and himself. Phoebe stayed with him for four days, spending much time "upon the beach . . . wading and digging, and 'as happy as a bird upon the wing.'" Dodgson wrote after she left: "I am rather lonely now she is gone. She is a very sweet child, and a thoughtful child, too. . . . Of course, there isn't *much* companionship possible, after all, between an old man's mind and a little child's, but what there is is sweet—and wholesome, I think."

Perhaps in his loneliness, Dodgson thought back to his younger days and contemplated his past friendship with Alice Liddell. Late in his life he wrote to Alice, who had long since been married and had become Mrs. Hargreaves: "I am getting to feel what an old man's failing memory is, as to recent events and new friends . . . but my mental picture is as vivid as ever, of one who was, through so many years, my ideal child-friend. I have had scores of child-friends since your time: but they have been quite a different thing."

During the period of that special friendship, Dodgson, in his early thirties, had become good friends with Alice's brother and later with Alice and her sisters. Together they played croquet and backgammon. The children visited him in his rooms and enjoyed his toys and books, but the activity they loved best was the boat trips they took on the river. Dodgson would supply a large basket of cakes or a picnic of biscuits and ginger beer or chicken salad, and they would row a boat to Nuneham, where they could eat lunch in the shade of a picnic hut. Dodgson always invited another man to help with the rowing, and the children's favorite was

Robinson Duckworth, who added to their songs with his fine singing voice. On these trips, Alice learned how to handle a boat and how to "feather" her oars properly.

On one occasion when Dodgson's two sisters came to visit and they joined Alice, her sisters, Dodgson, and Duckworth for a picnic, the boating trip ended with dampened spirits. In the midst of the expedition, they were caught in a torrent of rain and had to make their way to shore. They tried to manage on foot but were soon soaked to the skin. Dodgson fortunately knew people living nearby, who gave the women and children shelter. Dodgson and Duckworth continued on, however, in search of transportation to convey them all back to Oxford.

Hoping for better weather, Dodgson planned another picnic. On July 4, 1862, in the afternoon, Alice, Lorina, and Edith, and Robinson Duckworth, joined Dodgson for another excursion on the river. It proved to be the most memorable trip the group ever made.

V. Stories

"Tell us a story!" said the March Hare.

"Yes, please do!" pleaded Alice.

"And be quick about it," added the Hatter, "or you'll be asleep again before it's done."

"Once upon a time there were three little sisters," the Dormouse began in a great hurry; "and their names were Elsie, Lacie, and Tillie; and they lived at the bottom of a well—"

—*Alice's Adventures in Wonderland*

Many years later, Alice described the events of that afternoon in July:

> The sun was so hot we landed in meadows down the river, deserting the boat to take refuge in the only bit of shade to be found, which was under a newly made hayrick. Here from all three of us, my sisters and myself, came the old petition, "Tell us a story," and Mr. Dodgson (that is Lewis Carroll) began it.

· Dodgson could begin a story anytime he had an audience, and certainly the three Liddell girls were eagerly attentive. They listened and were wrapped in the spell of the story as Dodgson told for the first time the unforgettable tale of Alice's adventures. Many years later, Dodgson recalled "distinctly" how "in a desperate attempt to strike out some new line of fairy-lore, I had sent my heroine straight down a rabbit-hole, to begin with, without the least idea what was to happen afterwards."

He continued the story in the boat, and Robinson Duckworth wrote later that "the story was actually composed and spoken *over my shoulder* for the benefit of Alice Liddell, who was acting as 'cox' of our gig. I remember turning round and saying, 'Dodgson, is this an extempore romance of yours?' And he replied, 'Yes, I'm inventing as we go along.'" When they had returned to Oxford and had escorted the children back to the Deanery, Duckworth remembered, "Alice said, as she bade us good-night, 'Oh, Mr. Dodgson, I wish you would write out Alice's adventures for me.' He said he should try, and he afterwards told me that he sat up nearly the whole night, committing to a MS. book his recollections of the drolleries with which he had enlivened the afternoon."

The historic day had ended, but a new adventure had begun for Lewis Carroll. He continued to work on the story he had told on the boat trip. He eventually made it into a book as a special gift for Alice, calling it *Alice's Adventures Under Ground*. Dodgson hand-lettered the words and illustrated the text with his own "crude designs," which he described later as "designs that rebelled against every law of Anatomy or Art." While he was finishing the illustra-

Dodgson's drawing of the white rabbit

tions for *Alice's Adventures Under Ground,* he gave a copy of the story to Mrs. MacDonald and asked her to read it to her children to see if they liked it and "thus to gauge its worth if published." Greville MacDonald wrote, "I remember that first reading well, and also my braggart avowal that I wished there were 60,000 volumes of it."

Encouraged by child and adult friends, Dodgson began rewriting the story for publication, and he engaged John Tenniel to do the pictures. Dodgson finished his own hand-made book and gave it to Alice in 1864. A year later *Alice's Adventures in Wonderland* was published, and innumerable children were introduced to Dodgson's remarkable storytelling powers.

The story of Alice's adventures was fortunately preserved in writing, but—in Dodgson's own words—many of his tales "lived and died, like summer midges." The original Alice Liddell remembered that

> he seemed to have an endless store of these fantastical tales, which he made up as he told them. . . . They were not always entirely new. Sometimes they were new versions of old stories: sometimes they started on the old basis, but grew into new tales owing to the frequent interruptions which opened up fresh and undreamed-of possibilities. In this way the stories, slowly enunciated in his quiet voice with its curious stutter, were perfected. Occasionally he pretended to fall asleep, to our great dismay. Sometimes he said "That is all till next time," only to resume on being told that it was already next time.

It is possible to get some idea of Dodgson's improvised stories from several letters that he wrote to child-friends. A story about three unusual visitors continues over three letters, two to Agnes Hughes and one to her sister, Amy.

Tenniel's drawing of the white rabbit

My dear Agnes,

You lazy thing! What? I'm to divide the kisses myself, am I? Indeed I won't take the trouble to do anything of the sort! But I'll tell *you* how to do it. First, you must take *four* of the kisses, and—and that reminds me of a very curious thing that happened to me at half-past four yesterday. Three visitors came knocking at my door, begging me to let them in. And when I opened the door, who do you think they were? You'll never guess. Why, they were three cats! Wasn't it curious? However, they all looked so cross and disagreeable that I took up the first thing I could lay my hand on (which happened to be the rolling-pin) and knocked them all down as flat as pancakes! "If *you* come knocking at *my* door," I said, "*I* shall come knocking at *your* heads." That was fair, wasn't it?

Yours affectionately,
Lewis Carroll

[?1871]

My dear Agnes,

About the cats, you know. Of course I didn't leave them lying flat on the ground like dried flowers: no, I picked them up, and I was as kind as I could be to them. I lent them a portfolio for a bed—they wouldn't have been comfortable in a real bed, you know: they were too thin—but they were *quite* happy between the sheets of blotting-paper—and each of them had a pen-wiper for a pillow. Well, then I went to bed: but first I lent them the three dinner-bells, to ring if they wanted anything in the night.

You know I have *three* dinner-bells—the first (which is the largest) is rung when dinner is *nearly* ready; the second (which is rather larger) is rung when it is quite ready; and the third (which is as large as the other two put together) is rung all the time I am at dinner. Well, I told them they might ring if they happened to want anything—and, as they rang *all* the bells *all* night, I suppose they did want something or other, only I was too sleepy to attend to them.

In the morning I gave them some rat-tail jelly and buttered mice for breakfast, and they were as discontented as they could be. They wanted some boiled pelican, but of course I knew it wouldn't be good for them. So all I said was "Go to Number Two, Finborough Road, and ask for Agnes Hughes, and if it's *really* good for you, she'll give you some." Then I shook hands with them all, and wished them all goodbye, and drove them up the chimney. They seemed very sorry to go, and they took the bells and the portfolio with them. I didn't find this out till after they had gone, and then I was sorry too, and wished for them back again. What do I mean by "them"? Never mind. . . .

Your affectionate friend,
Lewis Carroll

Agnes's sister heard more about the cats in her letter from Dodgson:

[?1871]

My dear Amy,

. . . You asked me after those three cats. Ah! The dear creatures! Do you know, ever since that night they first came, they have *never left me*? Isn't it kind of them? Tell Agnes this. She will be interested to hear it. And they *are* so kind and thoughtful! Do you know, when I had gone out for a walk the other day, they got *all* my books out of the bookcase, and opened them on the floor, to be ready for me to read. They opened them all at page 50, because they thought that would be a nice useful page to begin at. It was rather unfortunate, though: because they took my bottle of gum, and tried to gum pictures upon the ceiling (which they thought would please me), and by accident they spilt a quantity of it all over the books. So when they were shut up and put by, the leaves all stuck together, and I can never read page 50 again in any of them!

However, they meant it very kindly, so I wasn't angry. I gave them each a spoonful of ink as a treat; but they were ungrateful for that, and made dreadful faces. But, of course, as it was given them as a treat, they had to drink it. One of them has turned black since: it was a white cat to begin with. . . .

> Yours affectionately,
> C. L. Dodgson

Gertrude Chataway had very fond memories of Dodgson's stories, and she wrote:

> One thing that made his stories particularly charming to a child was that he often took his cue from her remarks—a question would set him off on quite a new trail of ideas, so that one felt that one had somehow helped to make the story, and it seemed a personal possession. It was the most lovely nonsense conceivable, and I naturally revelled in it. His vivid imagination would fly from one subject to another, and was never tied down in any way by the probabilities of life.

No better evidence exists in support of Gertrude's words than this letter to Maggie Bowman. A note from Maggie sending Dodgson "sacks full of love and baskets full of kisses" brought this surprising reply:

. . . But how badly you *do* spell your words! I *was* so puzzled about the "sacks full of love and baskets full of kisses!" But at last I made out why, of course, you meant "a sack full of *gloves,* and a basket full of *kittens!*" Then I understood what you were sending me. And just then Mrs. Dyer came to tell me a large sack and a basket had come. There was such a miawing in the house, as if all the cats in Eastbourne had come to see me! "Oh, just open them please, Mrs. Dyer, and count the things in them!"

So in a few minutes Mrs. Dyer came and said, "500 pairs of gloves in the sack and 250 kittens in the basket."

"Dear me! That makes 1000 gloves! four times as many gloves as kittens! It's very kind of Maggie, but why did she send so many gloves? for I haven't got 1000 *hands,* you know, Mrs. Dyer."

And Mrs. Dyer said, "No, indeed, you're 998 hands short of that!"

However the next day I made out what to do, and I took the basket with me and walked off to the parish school—the *girls'* school, you know—and I said to the mistress, "How many little girls are there at school to-day?"

"Exactly 250, sir."

"And have they all been *very* good all day?"

"As good as gold, sir."

So I waited outside the door with my basket, and as each little girl came out, I just popped a soft little kitten into her hands! Oh what joy there was! The little girls went all dancing home, nursing their kittens, and the whole air was full of purring! Then, the next morning, I went to the school, before it opened, to ask the little girls how the kittens had behaved in the night. And they all arrived sobbing and crying, and their faces and hands were all covered with scratches, and they had the kittens wrapped up in their pinafores to keep them from scratching any more. And they sobbed out, "The kittens have been scratching us all night, all the night."

So then I said to myself, "What a nice little girl Maggie is. *Now* I see why she sent all those gloves, and why there are four times as many gloves as kittens!" and I said loud to the little girls, "Never mind, my dear children, do your lessons *very* nicely, and don't cry any more, and when school is over, you'll find me at the door, and you shall see what you shall see!"

So, in the evening, when the little girls came running out, with the kittens still wrapped up in their pinafores, there was I, at the door, with a big sack! And, as each little girl came out, I just popped into her hand two pairs of gloves! And each little girl unrolled her pinafore and took out an angry little kitten, spitting and snarling, with its claws sticking out like a hedgehog. But it hadn't time to scratch, for, in one moment, it found all its four claws popped into nice soft warm gloves! And then the kittens got quite sweet-tempered and gentle, and began purring again!

So the little girls went dancing home again, and the next morning they came dancing back to school. The scratches were all healed, and they told me "The kittens *have* been good!" And, when any kitten wants to catch a mouse, it just takes off *one* of its gloves; and if it wants to catch *two* mice, it takes off two gloves; and if it wants to catch *three* mice, it takes off *three* gloves; and if it wants to catch *four* mice, it takes off all its gloves. But the moment they've caught the mice, they pop their gloves on again, because they know we can't love them without their gloves. For, you see, "gloves" have got "love" *inside* them—there's none *outside*!

So all the little girls said, "Please thank Maggie and we send her 250 *loves*, and 1000 *kisses* in return for her 250 kittens and her 1000 *gloves*!!" And I told them [they had the numbers of loves and kisses] in the wrong order! and they said they hadn't.

Your loving old Uncle,
C.L.D.

Love and kisses to Nellie and Emsie.

Often Dodgson found inspiration for new tales in the toys or pets of his friends. The doll "Alice" who appears in this letter to Beatrice Hatch was a present from Dodgson. "It had fair hair brushed back from its forehead, just like the pictures of its namesake." "Emily" and "Mabel" were also dolls.

Beatrice and Ethel Hatch, about 1872

[Christel Church, Oxford]
November 13, 1873

My dear Birdie,

I met her just outside Tom Gate, walking very stiffly, and I think she was trying to find her way to my rooms. So I said, "Why have you come here without Birdie?" So she said, "Birdie's gone! and Emily's gone! and Mabel isn't kind to me!" And two little waxy tears came running down her cheeks.

Why, how stupid of me! I've never told you who it was, all the time! It was your new doll. I was very glad to see her, and I took her to my room, and gave her some Vesta matches to eat, and a cup of nice melted wax to drink, for the poor little thing was *very* hungry and thirsty after her long walk. So I said, "Come and sit down by the fire, and let's have a comfortable chat." "Oh, no! *no!*" she said. "I'd *much* rather not! You know I do melt so *very* easily!" And she made me take her quite to the other side of the room, where it was very cold: and then she sat on my knee, and fanned herself with a pen-wiper, because she said she was afraid the end of her nose was beginning to melt.

"You've no *idea* how careful we have to be, we dolls," she said. "Why, there was a sister of mine—would you believe it?—she went up to the fire to warm her hands, and one of her hands dropped right off! There now!"

"Of course it dropped *right* off," I said, "because it was the *right* hand." "And how do you know it was the *right* hand, Mister Carroll?" the doll said.

So I said, "I think it must have been the *right* hand, because the other hand was *left*."

The doll said, "I shan't laugh. It's a very bad joke. Why, even a common wooden doll could make a better joke than that. And besides, they've made my mouth so stiff and hard, that I *can't* laugh, if I try ever so much!"

Very Truly Yours, Charles L. Dodgson, Alias Lewis Carroll

"Don't be cross about it," I said, "but tell me this. I'm going to give Birdie and the other children one photograph each, whichever they choose. Which do you think Birdie will choose?" "I don't know," said the doll: "you'd better ask her." So I took her home in a Hansom Cab. . . .

Your affectionate friend,
Lewis Carroll

Dodgson's meeting with Alexandra (Xie) Kitchin's pug dog had been an equally interesting experience.

Christ Church, Oxford
August 21, 1873

My dear Xie,

. . . The day after you went, I passed by your garden, and saw the little pug-dog wandering in and out, and it turned up its nose at me. So I went up to it and said, "It is not good manners to turn up your nose at people!" Its eyes filled with tears, and it said, "I wasn't doing it at *you*, Sir! It was only to keep myself from crying." "But what are you crying about, little pug-dog?" said I. The poor little dog rubbed its paws over its eyes, and said, "Because my Ex—" "Because your Extravagance has ruined you?" I said. "Then let it be a lesson to you *not* to be extravagant. You should only spend a halfpenny a year." "No, it's *not* that," said the little dog. "It's because my Ex—" "Because your Excellent master, Mr. Kitchin, is gone?" I said. "*No!*" said the little dog. "*Do* let me finish the word! It's because my Exie is gone!" "Well! What of that?" I said. "She's only a child! She's not a bone!"

"No," said the pug: "she's not a bone."

"Now, tell me the truth," I said. "Which do you like the best? Xie, or a bone?"

The little dog thought for a minute, and then he said, "She's very 'bonne,' you know: that means 'good' in French. But she's not so good as a bone!"

Wasn't it an interesting conversation? . . .

> Yours very affectionately,
> C. L. Dodgson

Dodgson's letters contain the nonsense that children loved to hear from him, but the written words cannot convey the full enchantment of having experienced his stories in person. "Uncle Dodgson's method was more potent than he knew," wrote Greville MacDonald, "and it made him very dear to us. We would climb about him as, with pen and ink, he sketched absurd or romantic or homely incidents, the while telling us their stories with no moral hints to spoil their charm." Evelyn Hatch also wrote of how

A drawing by Dodgson

Dodgson would accompany his stories with vigorous illustrations:

Mr. Dodgson was no draughtsman, but at least he could make his figures full of expression in a few dramatic strokes—hair on end with fright, hands raised in horror, or faces broad with smiles. Every story had some unexpected and marvellous ending. There was the one which finished with the words: "My dear, you are a *Perfect Goose!*" and lo and behold, the drawing which had gone alongside the tale of a little man and woman who lived in a house with one window, by the side of a lake, and had been frightened by imaginary burglars, was turned upside down and there was a *Perfect Goose!* It was the way Mr. Dodgson told it, rather than the story itself, which always gave the never-to-be-forgotten thrill.

VI. Art and Photography

Alice . . . turned to the Mock Turtle, and said, "What else had you to learn?"

"Well, there was Mystery," the Mock Turtle replied, counting off the subjects on his flappers,—"Mystery, ancient and modern, with Seaography: then Drawling—the Drawling-master was an old conger-eel, that used to come once a week: *he* taught us Drawling, Stretching, and Fainting in Coils."

—*Alice's Adventures in Wonderland*

Although Charles Dodgson never had a drawing lesson, he had a keen appreciation for art and enjoyed illustrating, sketching, and photographing. As a boy he had accompanied his poems with pictures for the family magazines, and as an adult, his child-friends recalled, he would draw on any scrap of paper to illustrate the stories he told. He took an active interest in the illustrators who drew the pictures for his books. When Tenniel was working on *Alice's Adventures in Wonderland*, Dodgson made many suggestions and even went so far as to provide a photograph of a child he felt should be used as the model for Alice. Whether it was Tenniel or Dodgson who decided that Alice would have long, fair hair is unknown. But certainly the drawings of the fictional Alice do not resemble the original Alice, who always wore her dark hair cropped short.

Tenniel did not like to use models, and he found Dodgson an exacting author. After finishing *Alice's Adventures in Wonderland*, he consented to do *Through the Looking-Glass* only with reluctance. Working with Dodgson for the two volumes of *Alice* seems to have had a disagreeable effect on Tenniel, and he wrote, "It is a curious fact that with *Through the Looking-Glass* the faculty of making drawings for book illustration departed from me, and . . . I have done nothing in that direction since."

In addition to his interest in the illustrations for his writings, Dodgson was also fascinated with preserving the faces and forms of children in his own sketches and photographs. His sketches of children are usually awkwardly drawn, but they have a charm of their own.

Once he pretended, in a letter to Jessie Hull, age eleven, that he had been rejected by her art teacher, Miss Heaphy:

Christ Church, Oxford
February 1, 1882

My darling Jessie,

And how do you get on with Miss Heaphy? Any "scenes" yet? Any sulks? Any tears? I hope Miss Heaphy will not be offended at my copying out a few sentences from *her* letter about *you*.

Dear Mr. Dodgson,

. . . I am afraid your idea about joining Agnes and Jessie, so as to make a class of three, is quite out of the question. . . . Another reason against it is that your *style* of drawing would never suit the class: it would simply hinder them in making progress. When I tell you that Agnes is already decidedly better than Tintoret and Turner, and is *nearly* equal to Millais—and that Jessie (the pet!) now draws in a way that would make Raphael (if he were now alive) shake in his shoes—do you think, dear Mr. Dodgson, that *your* twopenny-halfpenny scrawls can be endured in the same room with *their* un-approachable pictures? The idea is simply absurd. . . . Yes, I assure you that neither Turner's, nor Raphael's, nor Titian's, nor Rubens' pictures are *the least like* what Agnes and Jessie can do! . . . The sweet Agnes at present inclines chiefly to houses. When I say "inclines," I write thoughtfully, for her houses *do* incline, it must be confessed, rather to one side: and the smoke from the chimnies [*sic*] is certainly *rather* solid: also her idea of a tree is at present slightly liable to be taken for a ball of worsted: but these are trifles. . . . Dear little Jessie pre-fers figures—children and animals: she nearly always gets the number of fingers and toes *quite* right: and as to

Very Truly Yours, Charles L. Dodgson, Alias Lewis Carroll

the animals, when once you have learned to distinguish which are cows and which are ducks, they are lovely, quite lovely!

There! Now I've given you a good idea what Miss Heaphy thinks of *you*. Now please (you or Aggie) tell me, with equal candour (I *do* like candid children—and sugar) what *you* think of *her*.

Whatever Dodgson lacked in drawing ability, he more than made up for it when he got behind a camera. For twenty-five years he was an avid photographer, and during this period he frequently invited children for photographic sessions.

Dodgson admired little girls (he thought that boys were "not an attractive race of beings"), and he was intensely aware of how quickly their childhood beauty passed. He wrote to a mother, "One reason for putting on record the faces of *children,* while you have the chance, is that in so *very* few years the *child*-face is gone for ever!" In wishing to photograph his child-friends, Dodgson found himself working against time, and often his invitations have an urgent tone. He expresses his fears in this letter to "Xie" Kitchin, one of his favorite sitters:

> I'm afraid it'll be another 6 weeks or so before I can invite you to bring Dorothy to my studio. *She* won't have grown too tall by that time: but I very much fear *you* will. *Please* don't grow any taller, if you can help it, till I've had time to photograph you again. Cartes like this (it always happens if people get too tall) never look really nice, as a general rule.

Dodgson's fascination with photography was in its early stages when he first met Alice Liddell and her sisters in the Deanery garden and helped to photograph them. Shortly afterward he purchased his own camera, and the Liddell children, who were attractive and willing sitters, made frequent trips to his rooms for photographic sessions. Alice recalled:

> When the time of year made picnics impossible, we used to go to his rooms in the Old Library, leaving the Deanery by the back door, escorted by our nurse. When we got there, we used to sit on the big sofa on each side of him, while he told us stories. . . . When we were thoroughly happy and amused at his stories, he used to pose us, and expose the plates before the right mood had passed. . . . Being photographed was therefore a joy to us and not a penance as it is to most children. We looked forward to the happy hours in the mathematical tutor's rooms.

Alice Liddell

Dodgson's methods show their success in Alice's pleasant, wistful expression.

In those days developing a photograph required a great number of complicated chemicals and procedures, which Dodgson describes in a poem called "Hiawatha's Photographing":

> Mystic, awful was the process.
>   First, a piece of glass he coated
> With collodion, and plunged it
> In a bath of lunar caustic
> Carefully dissolved in water—
> There he left it certain minutes.
>   Secondly, my Hiawatha
> Made with cunning hand a mixture
> Of the acid pyrro-gallic,
> And of glacial-acetic,
> And of alcohol and water—
> This developed all the picture.
>   Finally he fixed each picture
> With a saturate solution
> Which was made of hyposulphite,
> Which, again, was made of soda. . . .

Alice was curious about the entire process of Dodgson's hobby. Her recollections continue:

> But much more exciting than being photographed was being allowed to go into the dark room, and watch him develop the large glass plates. What could be more thrilling than to see the negative gradually take shape, as he gently rocked it to and fro in the acid bath? Besides, the dark room was so mysterious, and we felt that any adventure might happen there! There were all the joys of preparation, anticipation, and realisation, besides the

feeling that we were assisting at some secret rite usually reserved for grown-ups! Then there was the additional excitement, after the plates were developed, of seeing what we looked like in a photograph.

Ethel Arnold experienced the same wonder and excitement:

Photographing or being photographed in those days was no joke; and for a nervous child . . . to keep still forty-five seconds at a time was no mean ordeal. . . . But I never catch a whiff of the potent odour of collodion nowadays without being transported on the magic wings of memory to Lewis Carroll's dark room, where, shrunk to childhood's proportions, I see myself watching, open-mouthed, the mysterious process.

Surely not all of Dodgson's sitters were pleased with being posed and remaining still for the camera. A photograph of Marcus Keane shows that he, for one, would have agreed that the experience was "no joke"—although he was treated to a toy horse and probably to stories as well.

Marcus Keane, 1863

An invitation to be photographed might have read like this one to Mary MacDonald:

> My photographing studio on the top of my rooms is finished now, and I am taking pictures almost every day. If you come, bring your best theatrical "get up," and I'll do you a splendid picture.

Once Dodgson missed an appointment with Annie Rogers who came, as he requested, to be photographed. He wrote this letter as an apology:

[1867]

My dear Annie,

This is indeed dreadful. You have no idea of the grief I am in while I write. I am obliged to use an umbrella to keep the tears from running down on to the paper. Did you come yesterday to be photographed? and were you *very* angry? why wasn't I there? Well the fact was this— I went out for a walk with Bibkins, my dear friend Bibkins—we went many miles from Oxford—fifty—a hundred say. As we were crossing a field full of sheep, a thought crossed my mind, and I said solemnly, "Dobkins, what o'clock is it?" "Three," said Fipkins, surprised at my manner. Tears ran down my cheeks. "It is the HOUR," I said. "Tell me, tell me, Hopkins, what day is it?" "Why, Monday, of course," said Lupkins. "Then it is the DAY!" I groaned. I wept. I screamed. The sheep crowded round me, and rubbed their affectionate noses against mine. "Mopkins!" I said, "you are my oldest friend. Do not deceive me, Nupkins! What year is this?" "Well, I *think* it's 1867," said Pipkins. "Then it's the YEAR!" I screamed, so loud that Tapkins fainted. It was all over: I was brought home, in a cart, attended by the faithful Wopkins, in several pieces.

When I have recovered a little from the shock, and have been to the seaside for a few months, I will call and arrange another day for the photographing. I am too weak to write this myself, so Zupkins is writing it for me.

Your miserable friend,
Lewis Carroll

Most of the time, however, Dodgson was ready and waiting when his young sitters arrived with their "best theatrical 'get up.'" He liked to photograph the children dressed in costumes, such as

Xie Kitchin dressed as "Penelope Boothby," about 1875

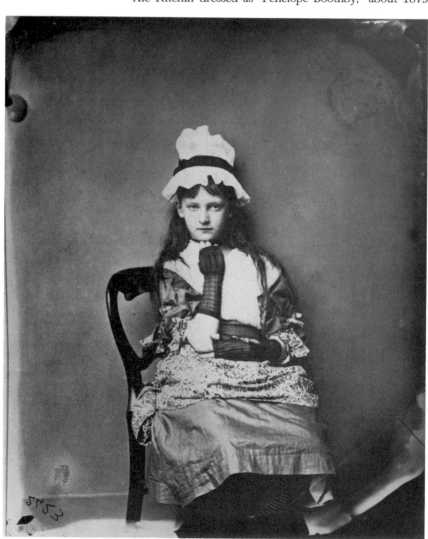

Xie Kitchin and her brothers as "St. George and the Dragon," 1874

beggar rags, Indian shawls, Greek dress, or Chinese dress. Ella Monier-Williams recalled:

> Although he had quaint fancies in the way he dressed his little sitters, he never could bear a dressed-up child. A "natural child" with ruffled untidy hair suited him far better, and he would place her in some ordinary position of daily life, such as sleeping, or reading, and so produce charming pictures.

"The Dream"

Dodgson exercised his love for the theater by staging a number of his portraits. Using a double exposure he created the photograph called "The Dream."

On at least one occasion a child was not enthusiastic about his ideas for special effects. Ella Monier-Williams remembered that

he was anxious to obtain a photograph of me as a child sitting up in bed in a fright, with her hair standing on end as if she had seen a ghost. He tried to get this effect with the aid of my father's . . . electrical machine, but it failed, chiefly I fear because I was too young quite to appreciate the current of electricity that had to be passed through me.

Naturalness in children always appealed to Dodgson, and he liked to see children at the seaside who were free of the stifling conventions of Victorian dress. Many little girls had to wear frocks to the beach, and Adelaide Paine remembered how grateful she had felt when Dodgson convinced her parents to let her play on

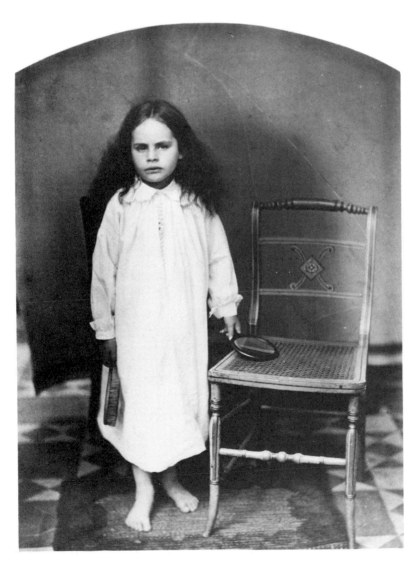

Irene MacDonald in
"It Won't Come Smooth," July 1863

Gertrude Chataway in her fisherman's
jersey and cap, sketched (right) and
photographed (below, right) by Dodgson

the shore without gloves. Gertrude Chataway, unlike most girls,
was allowed to wear suitable "wading attire," short bathing pants
and a fisherman's jersey. The mothers of other children were
shocked by Gertrude's outfit, but Dodgson approved of comfortable play clothes. He sketched and photographed Gertrude in the
fisherman's jersey.

Dodgson's desire to photograph the "natural" child extended
beyond the costume of informal clothing. As an artist, Dodgson
admired the child form and with punctiliousness requested permission from some parents to photograph their young girls without
clothing. When Gertrude was ten years old, Dodgson wrote to
Mrs. Chataway:

> If you should decide on sending over Gertrude and not
> coming yourself, would you kindly let me know what is

Very Truly Yours, Charles L. Dodgson, Alias Lewis Carroll

the minimum amount of dress in which you are willing to have her taken? With that information, I will then be guided by *her* likings in the matter: children differ very much—with some that I know (Londoners chiefly) I would not venture to propose even taking off their shoes: but with a child like your Gertrude, as simple-minded as Eve in the garden of Eden, *I* should see no objection (provided she liked it herself) to photographing her in Eve's original dress. And I think, if you were here and could see the photographs I have done of children in that primitive costume, that you would agree that it is quite possible to make such a picture that you might frame it and hang it up in your drawing-room.

But, much as I should myself like to have such a picture of her, if *you* at all object, or if *she* has changed her mind since I saw her (she was quite willing to be taken so, last September), of course I give it up, though I do

not, once in a hundred cases, get so well-formed a subject for art.

Mrs. Chataway apparently did not give her consent, but when parents did grant permission, the final decision resided with the child.

Nude photographs were Dodgson's final experiments, and in 1880 he gave up photography entirely. This hobby had occupied his time and energy for much of his life, but Dodgson seemed content to live without it, provided he continued to have the companionship of children. He wrote to Mary Mallalieu:

Christ Church, Oxford
November 11, 1891

My dear Polly,

I like the photograph very much, and I thank you for sending it to me: and also for sending me your love, which I like a great deal more than the photograph. Photographs are very pleasant things to have, but *love* is the best thing in all the world. Don't you think so?

VII. Poetry, Riddles, and Puzzles

"As to poetry, you know," said Humpty Dumpty, stretching out one of his great hands, "*I* can repeat poetry as well as other folk, if it comes to that—"

"Oh, it needn't come to that!" Alice hastily said, hoping to keep him from beginning.

"The piece I'm going to repeat," he went on without noticing her remark, "was written entirely for your amusement."

Alice felt that in that case she really *ought* to listen to it; so she sat down, and said "Thank you" rather sadly.

—*Through the Looking-Glass*

Taking photographs and drawing pictures were important means of artistic expression for Dodgson, but he showed his greatest talent when he created with words. Besides stories, he wrote poems, songs, and riddles and devised word games to amuse himself and his friends.

His fondness for writing poetry developed at an early age. By the time he was thirteen he had filled the first family magazine, *Useful and Instructive Poetry*, with nonsense verse to entertain his brothers and sisters. One of the poems in the magazine contains valuable advice:

RULES AND REGULATIONS

A short direction
To avoid dejection . . .
Learn well your grammar,
And never stammer,
Write well and neatly,
And sing most sweetly,
Be enterprising,
Love early rising,
Go walks of six miles,
Have ready quick smiles,
With lightsome laughter,
Soft flowing after.
Drink tea, not coffee;
Never eat toffy.
Eat bread with butter.
Once more, don't stutter.
Don't waste your money,
Abstain from honey.
Shut doors behind you,
(Don't slam them, mind you.)
Drink beer, not porter.
Don't enter the water
Till to swim you are able.
Sit close to the table.
Take care of a candle.
Shut a door by the handle,
Don't push with your shoulder
Until you are older.
Lose not a button.
Refuse cold mutton.
Starve your canaries.
Believe in fairies.
If you are able,
Don't have a stable

With any mangers.
Be rude to strangers.
Moral: Behave.

Sounding much like the Duchess in *Alice's Adventures in Wonderland*, who was "fond . . . of finding morals in things," Dodgson ended many of the poems in the magazine with such maxims as:

Moral: Keep your wits about you.
Moral: Never stew your sister.
Moral: Don't dream.

A number of family magazines followed *Useful and Instructive Poetry*, and throughout his youth Dodgson kept his free time busily occupied with writing poetry and prose.

In 1855, at the age of twenty-three, Dodgson wrote a mysterious stanza of poetry and copied it into his scrapbook, *Mischmasch:*

Dodgson called the words a "Stanza of Anglo-Saxon Poetry" and wrote:

This curious fragment reads thus in modern characters:

TWAS BRYLLYG, AND THE SLYTHY TOVES
DID GYRE AND GYMBLE IN THE WABE:
ALL MIMSY WERE THE BOROGOVES;
AND THE MOME RATHS OUTGRABE.

Seventeen years later Dodgson used these same curious lines, very slightly altered, to begin his famous poem "Jabberwocky" in *Through the Looking-Glass.*

A number of Dodgson's poems were written for special child-friends. When Alice Liddell was nine years old, Dodgson gave her and her sisters a book called *Holiday House,* written by Catherine Sinclair. He invented this poem and copied it on the inside cover of the book:

Little maidens, when you look

On this little story-book,

Reading with attentive eye

Its enticing history,

Never think that hours of play

Are your only HOLIDAY,

And that in a HOUSE of joy

Lessons serve but to annoy:

If in any HOUSE you find

Children of a gentle mind,

Each the others pleasing ever—

Each the others vexing never—

Daily work and pastime daily

In their order taking gaily—

Then be very sure that they

Have a *life* of HOLIDAY.

Perhaps Lorina, Alice, and Edith did not notice at once that their names could be spelled out with the first letter of every line, but they could not have missed *Holiday House,* which appears forward and backward.

Dodgson often heard the Liddell sisters recite poetry and sing songs. When they all went rowing together, Alice recalled, they "generally sang songs popular at the time, such as, 'Star of the evening, beautiful star,' and 'Twinkle, twinkle, little star.'" Some of the songs and poems appeared in *Alice's Adventures in Wonderland,* but with "the words all coming different." "Star of the evening, beautiful star" becomes, when the Mock Turtle sings it:

> Beautiful Soup, so rich and green,
> Waiting in a hot tureen!
> Who for such dainties would not stoop?
> Soup of the evening, beautiful Soup!

And the Mad Hatter's version of "Twinkle, twinkle, little star" is:

> Twinkle, twinkle, little bat!
> How I wonder what you're at!
> Up above the world you fly,
> Like a tea-tray in the sky.

When Alice's adventures were published, Victorian children found that Lewis Carroll's nonsense had made their songs and poems a good deal less familiar and much more fun.

---

1. Riddle: Why is a raven like a writing-desk?

(The answers to all riddles, word games, and puzzles will be given at the end of this chapter.)

The children who were most fortunate were able to recognize themselves in Dodgson's poems. He used this verse about Gertrude Chataway in the dedication to his long nonsense poem *The Hunting of the Snark.*

Girt with a boyish garb for boyish task,
    Eager she wields her spade: yet loves as well
Rest on a friendly knee, intent to ask
    The tale he loves to tell.

Rude spirits of the seething outer strife,
    Unmeet to read her pure and simple spright,
Deem, if you list, such hours a waste of life,
    Empty of all delight!

Chat on, sweet Maid, and rescue from annoy
    Hearts that by wiser talk are unbeguiled.
Ah, happy he who owns that tenderest joy,
    The heart-love of a child!

Away, fond thoughts, and vex my soul no more!
    Work claims my wakeful nights, my busy days—
Albeit bright memories of that sunlit shore
    Yet haunt my dreaming gaze!

Before publishing the poem, Dodgson asked for Mrs. Chataway's permission:

> Christ Church, Oxford
> October 28, 1875
>
> Dear Mrs. Chataway,
>
> . . . I can't feel sure from your letter whether you have or have not noticed that the verses embody [Gertrude's] name. They do it in two ways—by letters, and by syllables—the only acrostic of that kind I have ever seen. Will that make any difference in the leave you give to print the verses? If I print them, I shan't tell anyone it is an acrostic—but someone will be sure to find it out before long. In haste,
>
> Sincerely yours,
> C. L. Dodgson

2. Riddle for Gertrude Chataway: Why is a pig that has lost its tail like a little girl on the seashore?

When Margaret Cunnynghame asked Dodgson to write a poem, she received this answer:

No, no! I cannot write a line,
  I cannot write a word:
The thoughts I think appear in ink
  So shockingly absurd.

To wander in an empty cave
  Is fruitless work, 'tis said:
What must it be for one like me
  To *wander in his head*?

You say that I'm "to write a verse"—
  O Maggie, put it quite
The other way, and kindly say
  That I'm "averse to write"!

Dodgson admired poets and their work, and once he went to unusual lengths to acquire several verses of special interest. Dodgson was acquainted with Alfred Tennyson and became friends with his two children, Hallam and Lionel. In a letter to his sister Mary, Dodgson described the hardships involved in convincing eight-year-old Lionel to trade poems:

I went to the Tennysons, and got Hallam and Lionel to sign their names in my album. Also I made a bargain with Lionel, that he was to give me some MS of his verses, and I was to send him some of mine. It was a very difficult bargain to make. I almost despaired of it at

Lionel Tennyson

first, he put in so many conditions. 1st I was to play a game of chess with him—this with much difficulty was reduced to "12 moves on each side," but this made little difference, as I check-mated him at the 6th move. 2nd he was to be allowed to give me one blow on the head with a mallet (this he at last consented to give up). I forgot if there were others, but it ended in my getting the verses. . . .

3. Riddle for Mary Forshall: Do you know the way to improve children?

Dodgson's love for words led him to devise unique games to share with his friends. One of his popular word games, "Doublets," is described in a letter to Elisabeth Bury:

I enclose some *Doublets*, with which you may like to

occupy your idle minutes (if you have any). To solve a Doublet, you must change *one* letter only, in the first word, making a *real* word; then change *one* letter only in this new word, and so on till you get to the second word. The intermediate words are called "Links," and the whole thing a "Chain." The fewer the Links, the higher the Score. The rule for scoring is "Take the square of the number next above the number of letters in each word, and deduct 2 for every Link." Here, for instance, is a Chain for "Turn CAT into DOG."

```
CAT
COT
DOT
DOG
```

The score is "16 less 4": i.e. "12." . . . Proper names are forbidden.

Ursula Mallam wrote of playing "Doublets" with three other children during a visit to Dodgson's rooms: "We had tea in his biggest room. After tea we played writing games. We turned *Pig* into *Sty* and put *Pen* into *Ink,* sitting in two groups and changing the letters, racing with each other to finish first, all of it very noisy."

4. Here are "Doublets" for beginners to try:
   Drive PIG into STY in 4 links
   Make WHEAT into BREAD in 6 links
   Make HARE into SOUP in 6 links
   Cover EYE with LID in 3 links
   Raise FOUR to FIVE in 6 links

Another word game was called "Mischmasch." "The essence of this game," Dodgson wrote, "consists of one player proposing a 'nucleus' (i.e. a set of two or more letters, such as 'gp,' 'emo,' 'imse'), and in the other trying to find a 'lawful word' (i.e. a word known in ordinary society, and not a proper name), containing it. Thus, 'magpie,' 'lemon,' 'himself,' are lawful words containing nuclei 'gp,' 'emo,' 'imse.'"

5. Anagram for Enid Stevens: "Make 'dry one' into one word: . . . also 'scale it.'"

Puzzles were a favorite pastime for Dodgson, and he perplexed, frustrated, and delighted many a child with difficult questions.

6. Puzzle for a child named Sally:
. . . Tell Sally it's all very well to say she can do the two thieves and the five apples, but can she do the fox and the goose and the bag of corn? That the man was bringing from market, and he had to get them over a river, and the boat was so tiny he could only take one across at a time; and he couldn't ever leave the fox and the goose together, for then the fox would eat the goose; and if he left the goose and the corn together, the goose would eat the corn. So the only things he *could* leave safely together were the fox and the corn, for you never see a fox eating corn, and you hardly ever see corn eating a fox. Ask her if she can do *that* puzzle.

Dodgson could boggle the mind even without words. Here is a

maze that he drew for a Dodgson family magazine. Begin in the center and try to find a way out. It is possible to go under or over passes, but a player must not cross any of the single lines that block the path.

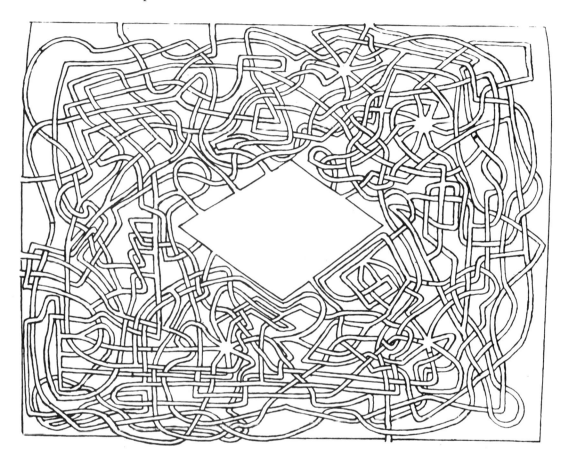

Not all children enjoyed the puzzles. Dodgson himself re-counted a disastrous attempt to set a puzzle for a new acquaintance, a little girl:

> It was at a dinner party, at dessert. I had never seen her before, but, as she was sitting next me, I rashly proposed to her to try the puzzle (I daresay you know it) of "the fox, the goose, and bag of corn." And I got some biscuits

to represent the fox and the other things. Her mother was sitting on the other side, and said, "Now mind you take pains, my dear, and do it right!" The consequences were awful! She *shrieked* out, "I can't do it! I can't do it! Oh, Mamma! Mamma!" threw herself into her mother's lap, and went off into a fit of sobbing which lasted several minutes! That was a lesson to me about trying children with puzzles.

One can imagine how Janet Merriman must have felt when she read this riddle from Dodgson: "'Why can't you make up *your* mind?'—that's a riddle I've just invented—'Because you haven't got one to make up'—that's the answer to it, only you'd never have guessed it." Dodgson undoubtedly knew that Janet would not find the riddle especially amusing, and he wrote this poem to explain:

"No mind!" the little maiden cried
   In half-indignant tone,
"To think that I should be denied
   A mind to call my own!"
And echo heard, and softly sighed (or seemed to sigh)
    "My own!"

"No mind!" the little maiden said,
   "You'd think it, I suppose!
And yet you know I've got a head
   With chin, cheek, mouth, eye, nose—"
And echo heard, and sweetly said (or seemed to say)
    "I knows!"

"You have no mind to be unkind,"
   Said echo in her ear:
"No mind to bring a living thing
   To suffering or fear.
For all that's bad, or mean, or sad, you have no mind,
    my dear."

Then if the friend whom you deride,
    To all your merits blind,
Should say that, though he's tried and tried,
    Your mind he *cannot* find . . .
'Tis but a jest for Christmas-tide, so, Janet, *never mind!*

Not all of Dodgson's poems are brightly nonsensical and teasing. His poetry can also be darkly melancholy, expressing a preoccupation with the death of the past. In the poem that follows, Dodgson hid the letters that spell Alice's complete name, Alice Pleasance Liddell:

A boat, beneath a sunny sky
Lingering onward dreamily
In an evening of July—

Children three that nestle near,
Eager eye and willing ear,
Pleased a simple tale to hear—

Long has paled that sunny sky:
Echoes fade and memories die:
Autumn frosts have slain July.

Still she haunts me, phantomwise.
Alice moving under skies
Never seen by waking eyes.

Children yet, the tale to hear,
Eager eye and willing ear,
Lovingly shall nestle near.

In a Wonderland they lie,
Dreaming as the days go by,
Dreaming as the summers die:

Ever drifting down the stream—
Lingering in the golden gleam—
Life, what is it but a dream?

ANSWERS TO RIDDLES AND PUZZLES

1. "Why is a raven like a writing-desk?" This riddle originally had no answer, but Dodgson later wrote one: "Because it can produce a few notes, tho they are *very* flat; and it is never put with the wrong end in front!"

2. "Why is a pig that has lost its tail like a little girl on the seashore? Because it says, 'I should like another Tale, please!'"

3. "Do you know the way to improve children? *Re*-proving them is the best way."

4. Charles Dodgson's solutions for "Doublets":

PIG	WHEAT	HARE	EYE	FOUR
wig	cheat	hark	dye	foul
wag	cheap	hack	die	fool
way	cheep	sack	did	foot
say	creep	sock	LID	fort
STY	creed	soak		fore
	breed	soap		fire
	BREAD	SOUP		FIVE

5. Anagrams: "dry one"—yonder; "scale it"—elastic

6. The man must make seven trips.
   1. He first takes the goose across.
   2. And then he returns for the fox.
   3. He takes the fox across and leaves it on the far side.
   4. And returns with the goose.
   5. This time he leaves the goose and takes the corn across.

Very Truly Yours, Charles L. Dodgson, Alias Lewis Carroll

6. With the fox and the corn together, he now returns for the goose.

7. Finally he takes the goose across to the other side and thus solves his problem. The fox is never alone with the goose, and the goose is never left with the corn.

7. Solution for maze:

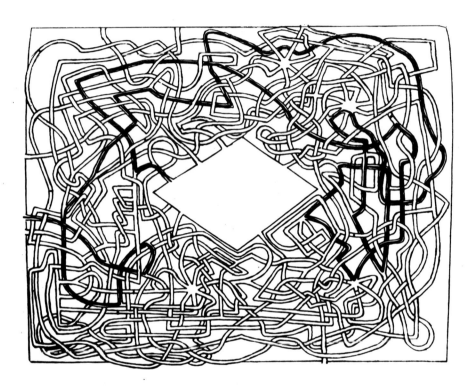

VIII. Lessons and Sermons

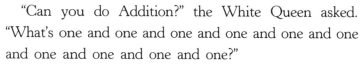

"Can you do Addition?" the White Queen asked. "What's one and one and one and one and one and one and one and one and one and one?"

"I don't know," said Alice. "I lost count."

"She can't do Addition," the Red Queen interrupted. "Can you do Subtraction? Take nine from eight."

"Nine from eight I can't, you know," Alice replied very readily: "But—"

"She can't do Subtraction," said the White Queen. . . .

"Can *you* do sums?" Alice said, turning suddenly on the White Queen, for she didn't like being found fault with so much.

—*Through the Looking-Glass*

Lewis Carroll, the poet, photographer, artist, and storyteller, cannot be separated from Charles Dodgson, the Oxford don and clergyman. Apart from entertaining children, Dodgson was also concerned with instructing them in mathematics, logic, and the Christian "law of love." As he grew older, his serious academic and moral interests became increasingly important in his relationships with children.

Dodgson's first biographer, his nephew Stuart Dodgson Collingwood, states that "children appealed to him because he was preeminently a teacher, and he saw in their unspoiled minds the best material for him to work upon." Teaching children was not always pleasant for Dodgson, however, and one of his earliest experiences teaching boys might have confirmed his preference for girls as friends and as students. Soon after becoming a Mathematical Lecturer at Oxford, Dodgson agreed to teach sums to a class of boys several times a week. He wrote in his diary of the first class: "I gave the first lesson there today, to a class of eight boys, and found it much more pleasant than I expected. . . . They seem tractable and in good order."

The next week Dodgson told a story that included sums for the children to work out. Things seem to have gone smoothly until the fourth lesson. Dodgson noted in his diary: "The school class noisy and inattentive—the novelty of the thing is wearing off, and I find them rather unmanageable." In the fourth week of instructing the boys, who continued "noisy and inattentive," Dodgson grew so discouraged that he decided to give up teaching the class.

The next year he tried tutoring Harry Liddell, Alice's older brother, but again the experience was disheartening: "My pupil Harry Liddell is beginning to tire of the Arithmetic lesson—today I could get him to do nothing." These unsuccessful attempts to

Harry Liddell

teach boys may explain the attitude he expresses in a letter written later in his life:

> To me [boys] are not an attractive race of beings (as a little boy, *I* was simply detestable), and if you wanted to induce me, by money, to come and teach them, I can only say you would have to offer *more* than £10000 a year!

Although boys proved to be difficult students, Dodgson decided that "girls are *very* nice pupils to lecture to, they are so bright and eager." During the later years of his life, he taught classes in logic to schoolgirls in Oxford and in Eastbourne, drawing puzzles on the blackboard and telling stories to make his lessons entertaining. A student at Oxford High School, Ethel Rowell, recalled her first impressions of Dodgson the teacher: "When Mr. Dodgson stood at the desk in the sixth-form room and prepared to address the class I thought he looked very tall and seemed very serious and rather formidable."

But the imposing lecturer soon won Ethel over to his fascinating "Game of Logic," and she became one of Dodgson's private students. She remembered how she went

> to and fro to Mr. Dodgson's rooms . . . and as the subject opened out I found great delight in this my first real experience of the patterned intricacies of abstract thought. . . . By his own real wish to know what I was thinking Mr. Dodgson compelled me to that arduous business of thinking, and to an independence of thought I had never before tried to exercise. . . . Gradually under his stimulating tuition I felt myself able in some measure to judge for myself, to select, and, if need be, to reject. . . . Mr. Dodgson at the same time bestowed on me another gift. . . . He gave me a sense of my own personal dignity. He was so punctilious, so courteous, so

considerate, so scrupulous not to embarrass or offend, that he made me feel that I counted.

Dodgson believed that logic is "one of the *best* mental exercises that the young could have," and apparently the logic of the "young" provided Dodgson with mental exercises of his own. He wrote to his sister Louisa:

Please analyse logically the following piece of reasoning.
Little Girl. "I'm *so* glad I don't like asparagus!"
Friend. "Why, my dear?"
Little Girl. "Because, if I *did* like it, I should have to eat
        it—and I can't bear it!"
It bothers *me,* considerably.

The children who wrote to Dodgson were sometimes reminded by his answering letters that they were addressing a mathematician, logician, and clergyman. Isa Bowman found that numbering hugs and kisses could lead to a complicated equation:

Christ Church, Oxford
April 14, 1890

My own Darling,
    It's all very well for you and Nellie and Emsie to unite in millions of hugs and kisses, but please consider the *time* it would occupy your poor old very busy Uncle! Try hugging and kissing Emsie for a minute by the watch, and I don't think you'll manage it more than 20 times a minute. "Millions" must mean 2 millions at least.

$$20)\underline{2{,}000{,}000} \text{ hugs and kisses}$$
$$60)\underline{100{,}000} \text{ minutes}$$
$$12)\underline{1{,}666} \text{ hours}$$
$$6)\underline{138} \text{ days (at twelve hours a day)}$$
$$23 \text{ weeks.}$$

I couldn't go on hugging and kissing more than 12 hours a day, and I wouldn't like to spend *Sundays* that way. So you see it would take *23 weeks* of hard work. Really, my dear Child, *I cannot spare the time.*

Why haven't I written since my last letter? Why, how *could* I, you silly silly Child? How could I have written *since the last time* I *did* write? Now, you just try it with kissing. Go and kiss Nellie, from me, several times, and take care to manage it so as to have kissed her *since the last time* you *did* kiss her. Now go back to your place, and I'll question you.

"Have you kissed her several times?"

"Yes, darling Uncle."

"What o'clock was it when you gave her the *last* kiss?"

"5 minutes past 10, Uncle."

"Very well. Now, have you kissed her *since?*"

"Well—I—ahem ahem! ahem! (Excuse me, Uncle, I've got a bad cough.) I—think that—I—that is, you, know, I—"

"Yes, I see! 'Isa' begins with 'I,' and it seems to me as if she was going to *end* with 'I,' *this* time!" . . . Please give my kindest regards to your mother, and $\frac{1}{2}$ of a kiss to Nellie, and $\frac{1}{200}$ of a kiss to Emsie, and $\frac{1}{2000000}$ of a kiss to yourself. So, with fondest love, I am, my darling,

Your loving Uncle,

C. L. Dodgson

P.S. I've thought about that little prayer you asked me to write for Nellie and Emsie. But I would like, first, to have the words of the one I wrote for *you,* and the words of what they *now* say, if they say any. And then I will pray to our Heavenly Father to help me to write a prayer that will be really fit for them to use.

Giving spiritual instruction and example to his friends was

deeply important to the Reverend Charles Dodgson. His Christian beliefs were the solemn reality of his life, and he tolerated no jesting on doctrinal matters such as baptism or the soul. When he attended plays with children and encountered dialogue or actions that he considered objectionable, he was quick to write letters of protest to the theater. The actress Ellen Terry, one of his best-loved friends, was not exempt from his criticism. She wrote in her memoirs that

> Mr. Dodgson . . . once brought a little girl to see me in "Faust." He wrote and told me that she had said (where Margaret begins to undress): "Where is it going to stop?" and that perhaps, in consideration of the fact that it could affect a mere child disagreeably, I ought to alter my business!
>
> I had known dear Mr. Dodgson for years and years. He was as fond of me as he could be of any one over the age of ten, but I was *furious*. "I thought you only knew *nice* children," was all the answer I gave him. . . . But I felt ashamed and shy whenever I played that scene.

Dodgson's concern for the spiritual education of his child-friends grew to occupy his attention more and more through the years. His first books for children, unlike most children's stories written before and during the Victorian era, are blissfully free of any morals and lessons that can be taken seriously. The Alice books, Dodgson wrote, "have no religious teaching whatever in them—in fact, they do not teach anything at all." In *The Hunting of the Snark* Dodgson was equally indifferent to teaching morals. To answer questions about the meaning of the Snark, he wrote: "I'm very much afraid I didn't mean anything but nonsense! . . . So, whatever good meanings are in the book, I'm very glad to accept as the meaning of the book." But as he grew older, Dodgson felt he should pursue his obligations as a teacher of the spirit, and his need to communicate his beliefs eventually appeared more strongly in his writings.

Sylvie and Bruno (1889) and *Sylvie and Bruno Concluded* (1893) were designed to express his moral values. He wrote:

> In *Sylvie and Bruno* I took courage to introduce, what I had entirely avoided in the two *Alice* books, some reference to subjects which are after all the *only* subjects of real interest in life; subjects which are so intimately bound up with every topic of human interest, that it needs more effort to avoid them than to touch on them. And I felt that such a book was more suitable to a clerical writer than one of mere fun.
>
> I hope I have not offended many . . . by putting scenes of mere fun, and talk about God, into the same book.

Dodgson also had hopes that were never realized of editing a child's Bible and of making a selection of Shakespeare's plays suitable for girls by "relentlessly erasing all that is unsuitable on the score of reverence or decency."

For the children who visited Dodgson at Eastbourne, morning lessons included Bible readings, and during the last year of his life a number of children heard his "lessons" in church:

> Last Sunday week I tried a novel experiment. For the first time in my life, I was asked to address *children*—at the "Children's Service" at Christ Church. It was an *extremely* interesting task. There were about 100 boys and 200 girls. I took no text, but merely told them a story (an allegory I devised years ago), with a *very* few words of explanation. It took about 20 minutes. I had to leave it unfinished, and went and told them another piece last Sunday. And *still* it is unfinished. It grows on my hands.

Dodgson continued to speak at children's services at Christ

Church and at Eastbourne. One sermon-story that is preserved in print describes the dream of a girl named Margaret who wants above all else to be loving and kind. She does what she can to help a lark, a rosebush, a baby, and a brown bird, and when Margaret falls sick and begins to die, she is revived by those whom she has helped. Margaret and her dream have little, if anything, in common with the indestructible Alice and her outspoken acquaintances of Wonderland. The sermon concludes with a message of grave importance to Dodgson:

> And now, dear children, I want you to promise me that you will each one try, every day, to do some loving act of kindness for others. Perhaps you have never really tried before; will you begin to-day . . . begin quite fresh to try your very best, every day, to do what you can towards fulfilling God's law of love.

Giving kindness and love to others as a means of gaining personal happiness was Dodgson's "philosophy" of life. He gave abundantly and received the pleasures of returned affection from the children he knew. He considered it "one of the deep secrets of Life," as he wrote to Ellen Terry, to know that all "that is really *worth* the doing, is what we do for *others*." Against the possible charge of selfishness, he continued:

> It is *not* selfishness, that my own pleasure should be *a* motive so long as it is not *the* motive that would outweigh the other, if the two came into collision. The "selfish man" is he who would still do the thing, even if it harmed others, so long as it gave *him* pleasure: the "unselfish man" is he who would still do the thing, even if it gave him no pleasure, so long as it pleased *others*. But, when both motives pull together, the "unselfish man" is *still* the unselfish man, even though his own pleasure *is*

one of his motives! I am very sure that God takes real *pleasure* in seeing his children happy! And, when I read such words as "looking unto Jesus, the author and finisher of our faith, who *for the joy that was set before him* endured the cross," I believe them to be *literally true.*

Giving and receiving between adult and child formed a meaningful, memorable bond between Dodgson and his child-friends, but it was a bond that, in many cases, could not last.

Very Truly Yours, Charles L. Dodgson, Alias Lewis Carroll

IX. "And Now the Tale Is Done"

As the Knight sang the last words of the ballad, he gathered up the reins, and turned his horse's head along the road by which they had come. "You've only a few yards to go," he said, ". . . and then you'll be a Queen— But you'll stay and see me off first?" he added as Alice turned with an eager look in the direction to which he pointed. "I sha'n't be long. You'll wait and wave your handkerchief when I get to that turn in the road? I think it'll encourage me, you see."

"Of course I'll wait," said Alice: "and thank you very much for coming so far—and for the song—I liked it very much."

—*Through the Looking-Glass*

The poem introducing *Sylvie and Bruno* begins with these lines:

> Is all our Life, then, but a dream
> Seen faintly in the golden gleam
> Athwart Time's dark resistless stream?

And well might Dodgson ask such a question, for his life of friendships with children was frequently subject to a "resistless stream" of time. The friendships were wonderfully loving and fun but often dreamlike in their impermanence; many ended as the child approached adolescence and experienced natural changes in her interests and personality. In a letter to the mother of a child-friend, Dodgson wrote:

> It is very sweet to me, to be loved by her as children love: though the experience of many years have [sic] now taught me that there are few things in the world so evanescent as a child's love. Nine-tenths of the children, whose love once seemed as warm as hers, are now merely on the terms of everyday acquaintance. Those that have gone on I reckon among my reallest and truest friends.

The little girls who grew into proper young ladies under the strict propriety of Victorian etiquette brought Dodgson many disappointments. As the eager, curious, vivacious, and boundlessly affectionate girls were transformed into reserved models of young womanhood, they inevitably changed in their behavior toward their gentleman friend of childhood. Dodgson described the process of his lost friendships with a note of irony:

> Usually the child becomes so entirely a different being as she grows into a woman, that our friendship has to change too: and *that* it usually does by sliding down, from a loving intimacy, into an acquaintance that merely consists of a smile and a bow when we meet!

Dodgson's special "loving intimacy" with Alice Liddell underwent this same loss of intensity as she grew into maturity. By 1865, when Alice had reached the age of thirteen, she and Dodgson were already on distant terms. They no longer played croquet nor rowed on the river. Alice's days of stories, riddles, and puzzles were over, and Dodgson rarely saw his favorite child-friend, who was quickly becoming a woman. A note in his diary reflects the strain in their relationship: "Met Alice and Miss Prickett in the quadrangle: Alice seems changed a good deal, and hardly for the better—probably going through the usual awkward stage of transition."

During this same period Dodgson was much involved with plans for the first printing of *Alice's Adventures in Wonderland*. Only three years had elapsed since he had first told the story to Alice and her sisters, but those past summer days had indeed become as a dream. Dodgson sent Alice a number of gifts over the ensuing

Alice Liddell, photographed by Julia Margaret Cameron about 1872

years—specially bound books and "Alice memorabilia"—and they remained cordial in their correspondence, but just as Alice's childhood had ended, so had the magic of their friendship.

Dodgson was highly sensitive to any change in the warmth of the letters or actions of his young friends. A letter to Agnes Hull, although humorous, shows his preoccupation with the probable shift in their relationship:

Christ Church, Oxford
April 21, 1881

My darling Aggie,

(Oh yes, I know quite well what you're saying—"Why can't the man take a *hint*? He might have *seen* that the beginning of my last letter was meant to show that my affection was cooling down!" Why, of course I saw it! But is that any reason why *mine* should cool down, to match? . . .) . . . I had turned it (half) over in (half of) my mind, the idea of calling at 55. But Common Sense said, "No. Aggie will only tease you by offering you the extremity of her left ear to kiss, and will say, 'This is for the *last* time, Mr. Dodgson, because I'm going to be sixteen next month!'" "Don't you know," said Common Sense, "that *last times* of anything are very unpleasant? Better avoid it, and wait till her sixteenth birthday is over: then you'll be on shaking-hands terms, which will be calm and comfortable." "You are right, Common Sense," said I. "I'll go and call on other young ladies."

While most of Dodgson's child-friendships ended on "shaking-hands terms," a few children grew up without changing their behavior toward him. "The *majority* (say 60 p[er]c[ent]) of my child-friends cease to be friends *at all* after they grow up," Dodgson wrote to a friend named Ada, "about 30 p.c. develop 'yours affectionately' into 'yours truly': only about 10 p.c. keep up the old relationship unchanged. It is a satisfaction to know that *you* are one of the 10."

As Dodgson advanced in years, he came to prefer the intellectual challenge and mature stability of friendships with young women. "Twenty or thirty years ago," he wrote in 1894, "'ten' was

Self-portrait of Dodgson, about 1895

about my ideal age for such friends: now 'twenty' or 'twenty-five' is nearer the mark. Some of my dearest child-friends are 30 and more: and I think an old man of 62 has the right to regard them as being 'child-friends' still." Gertrude Chataway remained close friends with Dodgson from her childhood onward, and she wrote of his insistence on having "child-friends," despite the reality of time's passing:

> I don't think that he ever really understood that we, whom he had known as children, could not always remain such. I stayed with him only a few years ago, at Eastbourne, and felt for the time that I was once more a child. He never appeared to realise that I had grown up, except when I reminded him of the fact, and then he only said, "Never mind: you will always be a child to me, even when your hair is grey."

Both old and new friends mourned when on January 14, 1898, Charles Dodgson died at age sixty-five after contracting a cold and developing bronchial symptoms. His illness was short, and his death came as a shock to his child-friends. Ethel Rowell wrote,

> It gave me a feeling of forlornness such as I had never known. . . . And there was nothing I could do as an expression of my sorrow—or so it seemed, till finally I hit upon an odd and childish device: I made a large badge out of some black ribbon I had by me, and I fastened this black badge to my petticoat in front just under my shirt blouse. I felt I could not wear the badge outside; people would ask what it was and after all he was no relation; yet I knew I must in some manner "wear black" for Mr. Dodgson.

But while Ethel mourned privately, the newspapers announced

Very Truly Yours, Charles L. Dodgson, Alias Lewis Carroll

his death far and wide with sorrow and with praise of his accomplishments. The *Daily News,* for example, recorded that "Mr. Dodgson was a man of genius . . . the two 'Alices' have never been superseded. It is possible that they never will be."

Dodgson would have been uncomfortable with the newspaper's praise and admiration. During his life he had answered laudatory letters with an explanation of his attitude:

> Please never again *praise* me at all, as if any powers I may have, in writing books for children, were my own doing. I just feel myself a trustee, that is all—you would not take much credit to yourselves, I suppose, if a sum of money had been put into your hands and you had been told "spend all this for the good of the little ones"? And besides *praise* isn't good for any of us; love is, and it would be a good thing if all the world were full of it: I like my books to be loved, and I like to think some children love me for the books, but I don't like them *praised.*

Although Dodgson would have disliked the tributes of his obituaries, he would have been especially pleased with the proposal of Audrey Fuller, a fourteen-year-old girl who had been a friend of his. She wrote a letter published in the *St. James's Gazette:*

> I have been wondering if all the children who knew and loved him, and the children who only knew him by his books, could not all join together and do some lasting good in remembrance of him. Perhaps we might collect enough money to have a cot in the Children's Hospital, and call it the *Alice in Wonderland* cot.

Money for the cot poured in from adults and children all over England. These were the innumerable children whom Dodgson never actually met but to whom he addressed Easter or Christmas letters enclosed in his books. One of those letters is addressed "To All Child-Readers of Alice's Adventures in Wonderland," and a portion of it indicates Dodgson's feelings of connection with his readers:

Christmas 1871

I have a host of young friends already, whose names and faces I know—but I cannot help feeling as if, through "Alice's Adventures" I had made friends with many many other dear children, whose faces I shall never see.

More than once he received a message of love from children who knew him only as the author of the Alice books. Dodgson found this child-love specially significant, because it was "so independent of all human acquaintanceship, and of all earthly meaning." He wrote:

I think the most precious message of the kind I ever got, from a child I never saw (and never shall see, in this world . . .), was to the effect that she liked me when she read about Alice, "but please tell him, whenever I read that Easter letter he sent me, I *do* love him!"

Dodgson treasured such a message far more than praise of his genius. He resisted the fame that had come to him except when it paved the way for new friendships with children. He wrote sincerely when he exclaimed in a letter: "I'd rather have *one* child-*friend* than a thousand child-*admirers*." The children who became his friends and found out what Mr. Dodgson was like discovered a uniquely brilliant man who loved children and childhood with untiring energy. They discovered a man with qualities that made it possible for him to write not only the timeless Alice books but also the following words, which conclude a letter to a new child-friend:

> Excuse my not signing "yours faithfully." I have known, in my long life, some 200 or 300 children, but, with nearly *all* of them, we sign to each other "yours affectionately." But please sign exactly as *you* like: only allow *me* to sign myself
>
> Your affectionate friend,
> C. L. Dodgson

Important Dates in the Life of Charles Lutwidge Dodgson

1832   Born on January 27 in Daresbury, Cheshire, to Charles and Frances Jane Dodgson.

1843   Moved with his family to the Rectory of Croft, Yorkshire.

1844–45   Attended Richmond School.

1846–49   Attended Rugby School.

1850   Matriculated at Christ Church, Oxford.

1851   Went into residence at Christ Church on January 24. Mother died on January 26.

1852   Received a Studentship at Christ Church.

1854   Bachelor of Arts degree.

1855   Became a Mathematical Lecturer.

1856   Photographed Edith, Alice, and Lorina Liddell for the first time on April 25.

1857   Master of Arts degree.

1861   Ordained Deacon.

1862   Told the story of Alice's adventures to Alice Liddell and her sisters on the "golden afternoon" of July 4.

1864   Completed the handmade book called *Alice's Adventures Under Ground* and gave it to Alice Liddell as a special gift.

1865   *Alice's Adventures in Wonderland* published.

1868   Father died on June 21.

1869   *Phantasmagoria and Other Poems* published.

1871   *Through the Looking-Glass and What Alice Found There* published.

1876   *The Hunting of the Snark* published, with a dedication to Gertrude Chataway.

1879   *Euclid and His Modern Rivals* published.

1880   Gave up hobby of photography.

1881   Resigned Mathematical Lectureship to have time "to do some worthy work in writing."

1883   *Rhyme? and Reason?* published.

1885   *A Tangled Tale* published.

1886   *Alice's Adventures Under Ground* published.

1887   *The Game of Logic* published.

1888   *Curiosa Mathematica, Part I* published.

1889   *Sylvie and Bruno* published, with an acrostic dedication to Isa Bowman.

1890   *The Nursery "Alice"* published.

1893   *Curiosa Mathematica, Part II* and *Sylvie and Bruno Concluded* published.

1896   *Symbolic Logic, Part I* published.

1898   *Three Sunsets and Other Poems* published. Died at Guildford on January 14. Stuart Collingwood, Dodgson's nephew, published the first biography.

Notes

"A TALE BEGUN IN OTHER DAYS"

p. 1   The title of the chapter is taken from the prefatory poem of *Through the Looking-Glass.*
"Dear Miss Dolly . . . Dodgson." November 28, 1867. *The Letters of Lewis Carroll,* ed. Morton N. Cohen and Roger Lancelyn Green (London, 1979). Unless otherwise stated, all letters in the text are quoted from this edition.
"Wrote to . . . was like." *A Selection from the Letters of Lewis Carroll (The Rev. Charles Lutwidge Dodgson) to His Child-Friends,* ed. Evelyn M. Hatch (London, 1933), 47.

p. 3   "Dear Lady . . . Sylvie." December 4, 1867.

I. CHILDHOOD AND OXFORD

p. 4   "precarious income." Letter from Charles Dodgson (CLD's father) to Rev. Dr. Bull of Christ Church, January 23, 1832. Quoted in Derek Hudson, *Lewis Carroll: An Illustrated Biography* (1954; reprint, London, 1976), 39.

p. 5   "even the passing . . . children." Stuart Dodgson Collingwood, *The Life and Letters of Lewis Carroll (Rev. C. L. Dodgson)* (London, 1898), 11.
"No one . . . fingers." Collingwood, *Life,* 13.

p. 6   "a wheelbarrow . . . truck." Collingwood, *Life,* 19.
"station master . . . assistants." Rules for the railway are in the Harvard College Library. See Hudson, 43.

p. 7   "I do not . . . genius." Collingwood, *Life,* 25.
"I cannot . . . again." Collingwood, *Life,* 30. A "public school" in England is a private boarding school.
"a muff." Hudson, 52.

p. 9   "My dear Henrietta . . . question). . . ." January 31 [?1855]. A "scout" is a college servant.

p. 10   "expression . . . hand." To Margaret Cunnynghame, January 30, 1868.
"Mathematical Lecturer." Although referred to as a "Lecturer," Dodgson had the same duties as a present-day "tutor" at Oxford. See *The Diaries of Lewis Carroll,* ed. Roger Lancelyn Green (London, 1953), 65. All diary extracts in the text are quoted from this edition.
"The friendship . . . or of men." November 7, 1896.

II. MEETINGS

p. 11   "[I] have more . . . fingers? . . .)." To Kathleen Eschwege, October 24, 1879.
"Sometimes they . . . altogether." To Edith Blakemore, March 31, 1890.

p. 12   Alice. Alice Pleasance Liddell was born on May 4, 1852, and died in 1934.

p. 13   "They were . . . I gave in." Collingwood, *Life,* 83–85.

p. 14   "A friend . . . Dodgson." August 22, 1869.
"quite by accident . . . delightful letter." Stanton I. Galpin, "Alice in Dorsetland," *The Dorset Yearbook* (1928), 46.
"elderly gentleman . . . From the Author." Hatch, 207.

p. 15   "Nellie remembered . . . and 'won't.'" Hatch, 208.

p. 17   "On one of our . . . *Alice in Wonderland.*" Harry R. Mileham, "Lewis Carroll," *The Times* (January 2, 1932), 6.

"Imagine . . . with his death." A. G. Atkinson [Gertrude Chataway], "Memories of Lewis Carroll," *The Hampshire Chronicle* (March 13, 1948).

"lived and died . . . midges." Collingwood, *Picture Book*, 165.

"he seemed . . . next time." Hargreaves, 6.

p. 52 "One thing . . . probabilities of life." Collingwood, *Life*, 380.

p. 53 "But how badly . . . Emsie." September 17, 1893.

p. 55 The dolls. Hatch, 83–84.

p. 56 Tom Gate. Tom Gate is the main entrance to Christ Church.

p. 58 "Uncle Dodgson's method . . . their charm." MacDonald, 16.

p. 59 "Mr. Dodgson . . . never-to-be-forgotten thrill." Hatch, 7–8.

VI. ART AND PHOTOGRAPHY

p. 61 "It is a . . . direction since." Collingwood, *Life*, 146.

p. 62 Tintoret. Dodgson has taken a liberty with the name of the painter Tintoretto.

p. 63 "not an . . . of beings." To Mrs. F. W. Richards, March 13, 1882.

"One reason . . . for ever!" To Mrs. C. F. Moberly Bell, October 13, 1893.

"I'm afraid . . . general rule." February 15, 1880. Cartes, as Dodgson uses the word, were photographic portraits mounted on cards and used by fashionable Victorians as calling cards ("cartes de visite").

p. 64 "When the time . . . tutor's rooms." Hargreaves, 5–6.

p. 65 "Hiawatha's Photographing." This is a parody of Henry Wadsworth Longfellow's *The Song of Hiawatha* (1855), which is well known for its distinctive rhythm. In Longfellow's poem, the Indian Hiawatha uses his skills in the forest. For instance, to make a canoe, ". . . he took the tears of balsam, / Took the resin of the Fir-tree, / Smeared therewith each seam and fissure, / Made each crevice safe from water." Dodgson borrowed the "easy running metre" to sing his own song of the photographer's life. He published "Hiawatha's Photographing" three times: In *The Train* (1857), in *Phantasmagoria* (1869), and in *Rhyme? and Reason?* (1883). In the 1883 version he omitted a section that included the lines quoted on page 65. In 1880 the photographing process had been simplified with the introduction of the dry plate, so this description of the collodion wet-plate method had become outdated. See Helmut Gernsheim, *Lewis Carroll: Photographer* (London, 1949), 113.

"But much more . . . in a photograph." Hargreaves, 6.

p. 66 "Photographing . . . mysterious process." Arnold, 783–84.

p. 67 "My photographing studio . . . splendid picture." May 11, 1872.

p. 69 "Although he had . . . charming pictures." Collingwood, *Picture Book*, 224.

p. 70 "he was anxious . . . through me." Collingwood, *Picture Book*, 224.

p. 72 "If you should . . . subject for art." June 28, 1876.

VII. POETRY, RIDDLES, AND PUZZLES

p. 79 "generally sang . . . little star'." Hargreaves, 7.

p. 80 "spright." An old-fashioned spelling of *sprite*, which means "spirit."

p. 81 "No, no! . . . 'averse to write'!" April 10, 1871.

"I went . . . getting the verses. . . ." April 19, 1862.

p. 82 "I enclose . . . are forbidden." March 8, 1896.

"We had tea . . . very noisy." *Letters*, 1115, footnote 3.

p. 84 "The essence . . . 'emo,' 'imse.'" This explanation appears in the printed rules for "Mischmasch," which was first published in the *Monthly Packet* for June 1881. Dodgson had first created the title *Mischmasch* for the scrapbook mentioned on page 77.

Puzzle for Sally. To Jessie Sinclair, January 22, 1878.

p. 85　"It was at . . . with puzzles." To Helen Feilden, March 15, 1873.

p. 86　"'Why can't you . . . *never mind!*" December 17, 1870.

p. 88　"Why is a pig . . . Tale, please!'" To Gertrude Chataway, December 9, 1875.

　　　　"Do you know . . . the best way." To Mary Forshall, March 6, 1879.

　　　　Solutions for "Doublets." Collingwood, *Picture Book,* 284.

　　　　Anagrams. To Enid Stevens, April 8, 1897.

VIII. LESSONS AND SERMONS

p. 90　"children appealed . . . to work upon." Collingwood, *Life,* 361.

p. 91　"I gave . . . in good order." January 29, 1856.

　　　　"The school . . . unmanageable." February 8, 1856.

　　　　"My pupil . . . do nothing." February 10, 1857.

p. 92　"To me . . . £10000 a year!" To Mrs. F. W. Richards, March 13, 1882.

　　　　"girls are . . . and eager." To Mrs. V. Blakemore, May 23, [1887].

　　　　"When Mr. Dodgson . . . formidable." E. M. Rowell, "To Me He Was Mr. Dodgson,"
　　　　Harper's Magazine CLXXXVI (February 1943), 319.

　　　　"to and fro . . . that I counted." Rowell, 320.

p. 93　"one of the . . . could have." To Mary Brown, August 21, 1894.

　　　　"Please analyse . . . considerably." September 1, 1897.

p. 95　"Mr. Dodgson . . . played that scene." Ellen Terry, *Ellen Terry's Memoirs* (New York,
　　　　1932), 141–42.

　　　　"have no religious . . . at all." To the Lowrie children, August 18, 1884.

　　　　"I'm very much . . . the book." To the Lowrie children, August 18, 1884.

p. 96　"In *Sylvie and Bruno* . . . same book." To C. A. Goodhart, January 11, 1892.

　　　　"relentlessly erasing . . . decency." Preface to *Sylvie and Bruno.*

　　　　"Last Sunday . . . my hands." To his sister Louisa, September 1, 1897.

p. 97　"And now . . . law of love." Collingwood, *Picture Book,* 343–44.

　　　　"one of the deep . . . *literally true.*" November 13, 1890. The scriptural quotation is
　　　　from Hebrews 12:2.

IX. "AND NOW THE TALE IS DONE"

p. 99　The title of the chapter is taken from the prefatory poem of *Alice in Wonderland.*

p. 100　"It is very . . . truest friends." To Mrs. F. W. Richards, November 23, 1881.

　　　　"Usually the child . . . we meet!" To Edith Blakemore, March 31, 1890.

p. 101　"Met Alice . . . transition." May 11, 1865.

p. 102　"The *majority* . . . one of the 10." To ?Adelaide Paine, January 9, 1884.

p. 103　"Twenty or thirty . . . 'child-friends' still." To Mrs. J. C. Egerton, March 8, 1894.

p. 104　"I don't think . . . hair is grey.'" Collingwood, *Life,* 380.

　　　　"It gave me . . . Mr. Dodgson." Rowell, 323.

p. 105　"Mr. Dodgson was . . . never will be." Quoted in Hudson, 19.

　　　　"Please never . . . like them *praised.*" To the Lowrie children, August 18, 1884.

　　　　"I have been wondering . . . *Alice in Wonderland* cot." Quoted in Hudson, 22.

p. 106　"so independent . . . earthly meaning." To Helen ?Feilden, April 20, 1877.

　　　　"I think . . . love him!'" To F. H. Atkinson, December 13, 1881.

　　　　"I'd rather . . . child-*admirers.*" To Gladys Langbridge, June 26, 1897.

p. 107　"Excuse my . . . Dodgson." To Nellie Davis, November 15, 1897.

Selected Bibliography

LEWIS CARROLL'S WORKS

The Annotated Alice, ed. Martin Gardner. New York, 1960.

The Annotated Snark, ed. Martin Gardner. New York, 1962.

The Complete Works of Lewis Carroll. London, 1939.

The Diaries of Lewis Carroll, ed. Roger Lancelyn Green. Two volumes. London, 1953.

The Letters of Lewis Carroll, ed. Morton N. Cohen and Roger Lancelyn Green. Two volumes. London, 1979.

The Lewis Carroll Picture Book, ed. Stuart Dodgson Collingwood. London, 1899.

The Rectory Umbrella and Mischmasch, ed. Florence Milner. Cambridge, Massachusetts, 1932.

A Selection from the Letters of Lewis Carroll (The Rev. Charles Lutwidge Dodgson) to His Child-Friends, ed. Evelyn M. Hatch. London, 1933.

Useful and Instructive Poetry. London, 1954.

The Wasp in a Wig: A "Suppressed" Episode of Through the Looking-Glass and What Alice Found There, ed. Martin Gardner. New York, 1977.

BIOGRAPHICAL WORKS

Bowman, Isa. *The Story of Lewis Carroll.* London, 1899. Reprinted as *Lewis Carroll as I Knew Him.* New York, 1972.

Collingwood, Stuart Dodgson. *The Life and Letters of Lewis Carroll (Rev. C. L. Dodgson).* London, 1898.

Hargreaves, Alice and Caryl. "Alice's Recollections of Carrollian Days, As Told to Her Son." *Cornhill Magazine,* n.s. LXXIII (1932), 1–12.

Hudson, Derek. *Lewis Carroll: An Illustrated Biography.* 1954. Reprint, London, 1976.

Wood, James Playstead. *The Snark Was a Boojum: A Life of Lewis Carroll.* New York, 1966.

WORKS WITH PUZZLES AND GAMES

The Magic of Lewis Carroll, ed. John Fisher. New York, 1973.

Gardner, Martin. *The Snark Puzzle Book.* New York, 1973.

Index

Page numbers in *italics*
indicate illustrations